The Book of Revelation

Question by Question

The Book of Revelation

Question by Question

Susan Fournier Mathews

Paulist Press
New York/Mahwah, NJ

Cover and book design by Lynn Else

Library of Congress Cataloging-in-Publication Data

Mathews, Susan Fournier.
   The book of Revelation : question by question / Susan Fournier Mathews.
      p. cm.
   Includes bibliographical references (p.   ).
   ISBN 978-0-8091-4585-0 (alk. paper)
   1. Bible. N.T. Revelation—Textbooks. I. Title.
   BS2825.55.M28 2009
   228.0071—dc22

                                                              2008046303

Published by Paulist Press
997 Macarthur Boulevard
Mahwah, New Jersey 07430

www.paulistpress.com

Printed and bound in the
United States of America

Contents

Contents

For Ed, with love,
and
For my father, in memoriam

Acknowledgments

I would like to thank my husband for the countless ways he supported me while I wrote this book. His own dedication to scholarship has been a genuine inspiration to me over the years.

I am also deeply grateful to the Capuchin Sisters of Nazareth for their reading through the Book of Revelation with me, but most particularly for their constant prayerful support, encouragement, and fraternity while completing this commentary.

A special word of thanks goes to the many students in my Book of Revelation classes, without whom I would have undoubtedly finished much sooner, but without whom my reading of the Apocalypse would be "flat," because it is from them I have learned to shape the questions that need to be asked of this intriguing text.

A great debt of gratitude goes to the Catholic Biblical Association of America for grants that funded much of the research and writing out of which this commentary sprung.

In addition, I must also thank the University of Scranton for funding that enabled me to make good progress on various stages of this project. Of my Scranton colleagues I am especially grateful to Linda, whose weekly conversations over coffee were a significant motivating factor for me in this labor. Lastly, I wish to thank Rev. Lawrence Boadt, CSP, for inviting me to contribute the Revelation volume to this new series, and for his patience in awaiting its completion.

Preface

This study guide for the Book of Revelation is part of a new series designed to assist groups or individuals who want to learn about sacred scripture at their own pace. This series provides commentaries that are decidedly different from other series. Instead of the typical line-by-line technical exposition, this series is built around the Socratic method of learning by question and answer. Like other commentaries, this study guide for Revelation will present the best of modern biblical scholarship in a methodological way, but unlike other commentaries, it will do so in a way more suitable for the classroom and study groups. This series aims more at a "hands on" practical approach by helping the student of the Book of Revelation to grapple with the text (in translation) by approaching it with probing questions. This book, *The Book of Revelation: Question by Question*, is a user-friendly guide to reading and understanding the last and most enigmatic book of the Bible.

The question-and-answer format is meant to help study groups understand and experience sacred scripture in a more effective way than the traditional academic commentary provides. The question-and-answer format is designed to help the reader learn to ask the right questions of the biblical text and in this way acquire the most advantageous approach to its study. A teacher can always tell how well his or her students grasp the material by the kinds of questions they ask. Teaching them how to ask the best, both useful and right, questions, is also teaching them how to read a text closely and fruitfully. Naturally, helping students and other study groups do so with scripture is rewarding for student and teacher alike.

The conclusions in each section are specifically intended to help the reader assimilate the material raised by the questions and provided by the answers. The reviews especially will assist the reader in drawing together the material in each section and coming to an overall appreciation of Revelation's themes and major theological ideas. The sections build on one another as the commentary progresses. The "virtual classroom" style of this series will make it ideal for parish adult Bible study groups and college-level inquiry. Nonbiblical theologians and teachers of humanities will likewise find it a ready resource for understanding the Book of Revelation. Preachers will find it helpful for setting out the major ideas and theology of Revelation.

The Book of Revelation is a particularly difficult biblical text. The overall gist of the question-and-answer format is to provide the reader with a proper context and background for interpreting the book responsibly and profitably without getting bogged down in technical details. The general style in presentation in this volume is that of the classroom, which is well suited to the Socratic method. In this student-friendly, informal way, study groups and students of all kinds will find it easier to study, grapple, and grasp the meaning of the Book of Revelation. The focus of this commentary is on major theological themes and threads rather than on every verse or phrase. It is hoped that this commentary will help the reader appreciate the many mysteries of this mysterious book.

Susan Fournier Mathews

General Introduction

The patron saint of biblical studies and great father of the Western Church, St. Jerome, once wrote that "the apocalypse of John has as many mysteries as words. In saying this I have said less than the book deserves. All praise of it is inadequate; manifold meanings lie hid in its every word" *(Letter LIII to Paulinus, 9)*. Most modern readers of Revelation would agree with this giant among scripture scholars: that its meanings lie hidden, and that it is filled with mysteries, but that they would find it hard to praise John's work or to say perhaps even less than it deserved.

The Book of Revelation is usually considered to be, at the very least, a "sealed book"—impossible to understand; and at the very most it is usually thought to be a book of terrifying doom and damnation. To most clergy, preachers, teachers, and religious educators, the book is so full of exotic symbolism and fantastic images that the challenge of fathoming and explaining Revelation's spiritual treasures to others is better not attempted. It is usually the case that most homilists and catechetical teams will studiously avoid any reference to liturgical readings from Revelation whenever they do appear.

Each year, for example, on the solemnity of All Saints Day, I take note of what the homilist will make of the reading from Revelation 7. Many homilists seem to expound upon the Old Testament reading, the Gospel, and the psalm response and conspicuously avoid commenting upon the reading from Revelation. One wonders just what is so daunting about such a simple vision of the elect that an otherwise competent homilist will steer clear of it.

The Church has placed the Book of Revelation in the liturgical cycle often enough, in fact, that a fundamental knowledge of its basic themes should not be out of the reach of the average educated cleric or layperson. By placing it in various prominent places in the liturgical calendar (e.g., All Saints Day, Assumption of the Blessed Virgin Mary), the Church obviously finds value in

1

nurturing the faith-life of the people of God. So why do not more homilists comment on it? Is there no clear way to expose the faith and spiritual value of the book? If what 2 Timothy 3:16 says is true, namely, "All scripture is inspired by God and is useful for teaching, for reproof, for correction, and for training in righteousness," then Revelation must also provide something useful. Since there is no other book like Revelation in the Bible, its uniqueness is all the more precious. To ignore its contribution to the life of the believing and praying Church is like ignoring the value of the Acts of the Apostles, another New Testament book without a biblical parallel but which, like Revelation, is the biblical instance of its genre.

In my experience, most priests and other faith leaders (catechists, religious educators, and nonbiblical theologians) do not know even how to begin to interpret the Book of Revelation. It seems too that the intimidation imposed by the book's own imagery and symbolism is compounded by the popular American fundamentalist uses and readings of the book, which are strange and offensive to Catholics and other Christians. Catholic and mainline Christian clergy and faith leaders know that the fundamentalist reading of the book is somehow unsound, and yet they do not seem to be able to say exactly how it is, or, better, to offer an alternative reading. They seem to have thrown their hands up, letting the fundamentalists have this bizarre book. The danger of deliberately avoiding comment on Revelation when it appears in the liturgical cycle is the missed opportunity of providing just such an alternative reading that is consistent with the life of the believing Church.

The danger is especially urgent with regard to the young, who seem to be most vulnerable to fundamentalist readings of the Book of Revelation. As a result of being persuaded by anti-Catholic interpretations of the Book of Revelation (e.g., the Harlot is the pope), many young people may consider leaving the Church. Not only do most Catholics not know how to defend their faith, but they are unable to articulate for themselves, let alone for others, a Catholic understanding of scripture, including, and especially, the Book of Revelation. If asked, most Catholics would respond with admitted ignorance about the Book of Revelation's meaning. To be sure, the Book of Revelation is a difficult read even for most nonbiblical theologians and humanists. The secondary literature on the book is enormous, and the scholarly interpretative schools many and varied, so that it is a huge task even for the specialist to navigate Revelation's many waters. Add to all of this the popularity of the *Left Behind* series and it is no wonder that mainstream Christian and Catholic leaders throw up their hands. The many mysteries of Revelation then appear to be incomprehensible riddles, and the intimidated interpreter misguidedly resorts to approaching them as secrets to be decoded.

The purpose of this study guide is to help Catholics and mainline Christians—specifically educated laity, seminarians, preachers, religious educators, students, and study groups—to read the Book of Revelation in a sound way. The goal here is to provide an accessible alternative reading to the increasingly popular American fundamentalist interpretations. While there is no single Catholic or mainline Christian reading of the Book of Revelation, there is an ecclesial context and tradition in which the book has been read and should still be continued.

There are ways of reading the Book of Revelation that the Church has rejected, even in Jerome's day, and ways of reading it that offer a sound interpretation in conjunction with its usage in the liturgy and together with the faith tradition. My hope is that this book will provide an entrée into the world and text of St. John's Revelation, so that after reading and using this book as a guide for the nonspecialist to study the Book of Revelation, other works on Revelation can be read beneficially. It is meant to be a companion to such standard kinds of commentaries, not a replacement or, least of all, a rival.

So why, therefore, another commentary on the Book of Revelation? To meet a specific need, the Paulist Press series, The Bible: Question by Question, is designed to help study groups and individuals work through the biblical books at their own pace in a kind of "virtual classroom." This book is intended, therefore, as a guide that is neither too simplistic nor too technical, but one that can be used in tandem with the biblical text itself while providing basic and practical information from modern biblical scholarship in a student-friendly format. It is hoped this book will be a resource and guide for reading Revelation for nonspecialists who want to understand its major ideas and themes.

As readers work their way through Revelation at their own pace using this commentary as a guide, they will see that the presentation is divided into chapters and verses that are easily identifiable sections. Each section provides an introduction to the material, which is designed to consider what might be useful to know before actually reading the text. The questions are next. These are intended to help readers grapple with the text itself, particularly its contexts and meanings. The answers to the questions are given in a separate section at the back of this book, so that the readers can work through the material on their own first. Each section ends with a conclusion, which is intended to draw the material together. At major divisions in the Book of Revelation, reviews are provided that are designed especially to highlight the biblical author's theological themes and major ideas.

There are some wonderful, sound commentaries on the Book of Revelation. The interpretation presented in this commentary is rooted in the best of modern biblical scholarship on Revelation. In particular, I have relied on the important works of Richard Bauckham, Adela Yarbro Collins, Eugenio Corsini, Wilfrid Harrington, OP, Craig Koester, and Ben Witherington III. The classic texts of H. B. Swete and R. H. Charles have also informed my thinking on Revelation.

There are basically two ways of approaching the Book of Revelation: one is to interpret the text in a fundamentalist-literal way, and the other is to interpret it in a symbolic way. This may be putting it too simplistically, but the basic division is accurate. Naturally, each of these basic approaches has a spectrum of interpretive methods and perspectives. The approach adopted in this commentary is the latter one, typical of mainstream Christian and Catholic ways of reading Revelation and indeed of the sacred scriptures as a whole. Within this approach, this commentary interprets the text in the light of the contemporary situation of the original author, not our own day as in a fundamentalist approach, with an emphasis on theological themes.

Throughout this commentary the reader can expect that the historical and political background of the late first century will be constitutive to understanding aright the imagery, symbols, and perspective of the book. Understanding the literary and theological characteristics of this apocalyptic-prophetic text will also be essential. All of these various elements will be discussed in nontechnical ways and only to the extent that they help illuminate the meaning of the book, since this commentary is written not for scholars, but with the nonspecialist in mind. It aims at being a middle course between the highly technical and the very elementary commentaries, neither too deep nor too shallow. It is hoped that it will be a resource, then, for the preacher, Bible study group, catechist, individual reader, and others, who may not have either the time or the inclination to work through the typical commentary written for scholars. Perhaps preachers and other church leaders will find that this commentary fills the apparent gap in resources for preparing homilies and study groups on the Book of Revelation.

The reader familiar with the Old Testament will have a much easier time grasping the theological meaning of Revelation, and of interpreting its symbolism and language. Perhaps one reason modern Catholics find the Book of Revelation so difficult to understand is that they lack the appropriate familiarity with the Old Testament. In a classic estimate, Swete suggested that out of 404 verses in the Greek text of Revelation as many as 278 of them contain at least one allusion to the Old Testament (Swete's *The Apocalypse of St. John*, cxxxv). Revelation rarely explicitly quotes the Old Testament; it simply makes extensive use of its imagery, symbols, and language. Since this is the case, one cannot hope to understand Revelation apart from the Old Testament. Indeed, what John does in Revelation is present a Christianized reading of the story of salvation, drawing heavily on the language, themes, and prophecy of the Old Testament. John presents himself in this book as a Christian prophet who stands in the tradition of and on the shoulders of the giant biblical prophets. He understands his work to be prophecy with an apocalyptic outlook.

The apocalyptic characteristics of Revelation present the second major obstacle to the modern reader. If the Old Testament is unfamiliar, the apocalyptic style of writing is completely foreign. Apocalyptic literature was popular from 200 BC to AD 200, both in Jewish and Christian circles. A large part of the Book of Daniel is apocalyptic in character. The Book of Revelation is the only canonical apocalypse (the word used for this genre of literature), and it bears the typical characteristics. Apocalypses use visions, symbols (colors, numbers, etc.), and imagery to console and move their audiences. They have a particular worldview that includes the notion that God is in control of the universe and will act soon to save his people and defeat his enemies. Apocalyptic literature generally hopes for redemption in the end-days in the form of a heavenly reign, and awaits the salvation of God, who is Lord of History, and the coming of his kingdom in triumph. Like Old Testament prophecy, Revelation seeks to make sense out of contemporary events and history, but with an otherworldly eschatological emphasis. John's Apocalypse is thoroughly Christian, and so its characteristics are imbued with the perspective of what God has done, is doing, and will do, in Christ, on behalf of his faithful people.

We must recognize that John's apocalyptic-prophetic perspective, imagery, and symbolism were understandable by his contemporary Christian audience. The challenge to the interpreter today is to make sense of them in light of their original contexts so that they can be assimilated and rendered meaningful in our own context. John was writing from exile to the persecuted churches in the Roman province of Asia Minor. The emperor Domitian, who ruled the Roman Empire from AD 81 to 96, had launched an imperial campaign against Christians, putting them to death for their refusal to participate in the pagan religion of the state. John writes Revelation and sends it to the beleaguered churches to encourage them to remain steadfast and faithful to Christ. Knowing firsthand the rage and intolerance of the Roman imperial court, John frames his encouragement in terms of a cosmic struggle between good and evil. Apocalyptic thinking and characteristics were well suited to describing this battle and its ultimate outcome. Adopting Old Testament prophetic language and theology were likewise effective ways of encouraging his contemporary fellow sufferers in Christ.

If John were writing to the twenty-first-century American Church, his visions and imagery would have to be quite different if they were to be understood by that audience. Once the modern reader gets a handle on the apocalyptic perspective and its characteristics, and if the modern reader has some familiarity with major Old Testament themes, then Revelation is not so bizarre or non-navigable. It is my hope that this commentary serves to guide the modern reader toward gaining such a handle and acquiring the necessary familiarity, all with the ultimate goal of reaching the shore of fruitful appreciation of the Book of Revelation, a book abundantly rich with great Christian theology and themes.

"How to Use"—
Instructions for Individuals and Groups

Like the previous titles in the Paulist Press series, The Bible: Question by Question, this book is designed for individuals or groups who seek to read a particular biblical book slowly and carefully, using study questions, together with modern biblical scholarship. It is aimed at the educated lay reader, adult Bible study groups, college students, seminarians, and others interested in reading and learning more about the Bible.

This commentary is specifically intended to be read in close conjunction with the biblical text of the Book of Revelation. The text of Revelation is primary; this commentary is supplemental. The question-by-question format will aid students of Revelation in learning what to look for in this difficult biblical text, as well as help shape their own understanding of the perspective and content of Revelation itself. It is recommended that for ease of learning, the commentary be used in tandem with the biblical text, and that each reader use the same English translation as the primary one in this series (New Revised Standard Version). The Book of Revelation was clearly meant to be proclaimed in the assembly. Those studying this book, therefore, should pay attention to its liturgical use. John also intended to move his audience by his choice of imagery and symbol; those studying this book, therefore, should read the text aloud and let the images and symbols "work" on them.

Revelation is one of the most enigmatic of biblical books. This commentary attempts to help the reader work through the text in a practical, straightforward way. This is done by way of the question-by-question format in which less technical explanations and commentary proceed section by section, with a focus on the author's themes and major theological ideas. The goal is to help the reader "see the forest for the trees," after identifying some of the "significant trees."

Individuals and study groups should work through the biblical text and commentary according to the order of the sections presented. In this way the material is studied progressively, which will make it easier to assimilate the book's content and meaning, since each section builds on the previous. The overall aim of this commentary is to help the reader discover that the many mysteries of the Book of Revelation are illuminated by understanding John's use of great Old Testament themes and images, his perspective on good and evil, his symbolism for God, Christ, and the Church, and his theology of the kingdom of God.

Lastly, in studying sacred scripture, there is no substitute for praying with the text. The reader is strongly encouraged to pray with the Book of Revelation, so as to "hear what the Spirit says." For a proper and fuller understanding of the Word of God, scripture must be read in the Spirit in Whom it was written (see *Dei Verbum* 12).

On a personal note, I find the Book of Revelation to be so thoroughly christocentric and countercultural, especially relevant to Christians today, that its images and exhortations are a constant source of encouragement and comfort in my own daily struggle to follow the Lamb wherever he goes. Revelation presents a theology of divine providence that is saliently Christian and more and more pertinent to the Church awaiting the consummation of the kingdom of God. It also provides real insight into the cosmic struggle between good and evil, which is reassuring and valid. Hopefully, readers of this commentary will be aided toward a similar kind of personal appreciation of the Book of Revelation.

Questions

REVELATION 1—3

I. Prologue, 1:1–3: Title, origin, and purpose of Revelation

II. Chapters 1:4—3:22: Introduction and exhortations

    A. Epistolary-prophetic introduction, 1:4–20

    B. Letters to the seven churches, 2:1—3:22

The title, introduction, inaugural vision (1:1–20), and letters to the churches (Rev 2—3) serve to place the tribulation, kingly reign, and patient endurance of the faithful in the context of their life in Christ in the present corrupt "age." Christ is portrayed as the gloriously enthroned and powerful Son of Man (1:12–16), who intimately knows the trials and tribulations of each community ("I know…"). The description of Christ in both the inaugural vision and the seven letters assures the churches that he is their almighty king present among them in their trials. But they are also warned that his continuing presence is dependent on their fidelity to him (Rev 2:5). The exalted Son of Man gives warnings or promises according to each church's life and work as they contend with trials and tribulations from within (2:2, 14, 20; 3:2, 16) as well as without (2:9, 13; 3:9, 10). In each of the letters, Christ exhorts the faithful to endure by promising those who are victorious a full share of life with him in the kingdom to come. Conversely, he warns the faithful not to conform to evil and to give up compromising with it, calling them to conquer temptation to infidelity and be victorious in persevering in virtue. The faithful are not told that their distress will be alleviated (3:10), but rather are warned to endure patiently in Christ, all with the aim of obtaining their salvation.

As can be seen from the outline above, chapter 1 is easily divided into two parts: a short prologue that sets out the book's title, origin, and purpose (1:1–3), and a longer introductory section with characteristics of a letter (i.e., epistolary) that includes a prophetic vision (1:4–20). From 1:1 we obtain the title to this last book of the New Testament. The very first word in the book is *revelation* ("apocalypse"). The revelation (apocalypse) is "of Jesus Christ," an ambiguous expression: Does the revelation belong to Christ or is it about him? The text tells us that God (the Father) gave Christ the revelation, who then entrusted it to an angel, who in turn delivered it to St. John. This chain of handing down makes it clear that this apocalypse is something mysterious, hidden in God, that is now being made known (1:1). So it seems that the ambiguity may be an intentional double meaning: the revelation *is* Christ's, and it is also *about* him. The entire book will support this interpretation, starting already in its introduction in 1:4–20.

John's identity is not clarified. He is a servant of Christ, who bore witness "to the word of God and to the testimony of Jesus Christ, even to all that he saw" (1:2). This sounds like an apt description of the apostle John, the son of Zebedee. It is he whom the early Church (with a few exceptions) identified as this John. The apostle John certainly bore witness to the Gospel and to Christ himself (notice how the "word of God" is reminiscent of John 1:1–3, 14 and can mean both Christ himself and the Gospel) in his preaching and authorship of the Fourth Gospel. In doing so he likewise testified to "all that he saw," that is, all that he saw of Jesus' earthly ministry, passion, death, and resurrection (John 1:1–18; 1 John 1:1–4). It is for this witness that John was banished to Patmos (1:9).

The prevailing consensus among modern biblical scholars on the provenance of the book is that it was written around the year AD 95 from Patmos, a small island in the Aegean off the coast of Ephesus. The ancient tradition surrounding John the son of Zebedee was that he had been exiled there by Emperor Domitian because of his witness to Christ. Domitian had unsuccessfully tried to boil John alive in oil; when John got into the cauldron, it seemed to him as a comfortable rejuvenating bath. In his fury Domitian exiled him to the Roman penal colony of Patmos, where he later received the apocalypse, the revelation of Jesus

Christ. Like Nero (AD 54–68) who preceded him, Domitian hated Christians and persecuted them. Domitian's persecution was not localized to the city of Rome like Nero's, but rather extended through the Roman province of Asia Minor (it would be handy for the reader to consult a biblical atlas or a map in one's Bible of the New Testament world). All of the Christians in that province would have felt the threat of martyrdom and the pressures to compromise with the reigning culture. The seven churches named in chapters 1 to 3 are all situated within that province.

Domitian's persecution was more pervasive than Nero's, not just geographically, but also institutionally. Domitian had an entire governmental system in place to impose on his subjects, willing or not, the cult of the worship of Rome, its emperor, and its gods. Those who refused were usually imprisoned and, when unwilling to commit idolatry, beheaded by the sword. By this time, Christians had become distinct from Jews and thus unprotected by Roman law from the exemption granted the latter from having to participate in the idolatrous imperial cult.

The overall purpose of the book is to encourage his fellow Christians to do as he did, that is, to bear faithful witness to the Gospel and to Christ. He exhorts them throughout this book to be faithful, even unto death. He is a credible witness, having himself suffered so much distress at the Romans' hands (Rev 1:9). He is also fulfilling his commission of making known to the Church the revelation Christ gave him for that purpose. The opening verses of this work make it clear that God's purpose in manifesting this revelation of Christ is to show his "servants" (that is, Christians, and judging from chapters 2—3, both faithful and unfaithful alike) "what must take place" and how they are to attain to ultimate beatitude.

John's commission is not a private, personal message, but a prophetic one that must be given publicly to God's people (1:3). This John, whoever else he may be, is an early Christian prophet who faithfully proclaims the word of God given to him. Like Old Testament prophecy, the prophetic message is meant to be heeded by God's people (1:3). Also in the vein of Old Testament prophecy, John's message begins with an inaugural vision, that is, a vision that initiates his prophetic ministry. This vision is recounted by John in this introduction, after a short epistolary greeting. The book opens and closes in a letter format (1:4–8; 22:6–21). It makes sense for John to enclose his prophetic vision and the revelation entrusted to him in such a literary framework. It gives him a way to introduce and conclude his message with a personal mark, thus adding the weight of his own personal witness and authority to the message, especially if he is one of the Twelve. The letter was a favorite vehicle for the early Christians to communicate with each other, especially when there was a pressing problem (e.g., Paul's letters to the Corinthians and Galatians), and also a typical means for a leader to give advice when absent from his community. As is the norm in New Testament epistles, the short introduction in 1:4–20 is a keynote for the whole book. John sends greetings from himself and the Trinity, emphasizing that God now reigns supreme and that Christ is coming soon to claim his dominion.

John's inaugural vision (1:9–20) may seem bizarre and fantastic to us, but to the seer and his contemporary audience it would have been powerful and reassuring. John sees Christ in glory and majesty, as the king of the entire cosmos. He is depicted here in terms usually associated with God in the Old Testament, so as to drive home the point that he shares in God's power, authority, and glory. He is also depicted in a way all too familiar to the Christians living under Roman rule in the late first century. That is to say, Christ is depicted as a Roman emperor. In portraying the risen Christ this way, John, inspired by God who gives this vision, boldly proclaims Christ to be the true ruler of the world and the one to whom Christians owe their allegiance. True authority and power does not belong to Domitian, who himself is subject to God, but to Christ the Messianic King. The glorified, imperial Christ commissions John to write this revelation and to send it to the seven churches persecuted by the "fraudulent" Domitian.

The messages to the seven churches in chapters 2 and 3 logically follow John's inaugural vision. These messages follow a pattern, which helps the reader to see that they are for local communities but are not private: note that in each letter there is the prophetic saying for those with ears to hear what the Spirit is saying to the churches, showing that in each letter the other churches and the universal Church are likewise called to heed Christ's words. The fact that there are seven churches addressed also indicates that what is said to one church may be applied to the others, and to the Church in all times and places. The pattern can easily be seen in these general terms: Christ's address to the community; his words of consolation and/or rebuke; his call to repentance and/or fidelity; and his promise of reward to those who persevere in fidelity to him.

These seven churches were real Christian communities, located in the western part of the Roman imperial province of Asia Minor. They are listed in the order in which one would have traveled from one to the other. These letters seem never to have been circulated independently of the book. Similar to the letters of St. Paul in the New Testament, they give us a concrete picture of the daily life and struggles of Christians in that time and place. Christ says he knows the hardships and joys of all the churches, their faithful and unfaithful members, their works and needs. Christians in every time and place can be assured that Christ continues to know them in the same intimate fashion.

Section One:
Revelation 1:1–20

Introduction

This first section contains John's greeting to the local churches in Asia Minor, to which he writes and relates the revelation of Jesus Christ given to him (1:1–8). This vision of the risen and exalted Christ is important to the thrust of the book as a whole. First, 1:9 indicates that the author himself shares in the current distress that the Church is undergoing, along with his fellow Christians in the churches of Asia Minor toward the end of the first century. As such it sets the tone and indicates that the entire book is set within the context of the seer's being a "fellow sufferer." Both John and the Christians of Asia Minor are servants of Christ (1:1). John knows fidelity to Christ in his culture is difficult, and so he accepts his suffering and exile to Patmos, and encourages his fellow sufferers to accept their own burdens.

John receives his vision while he is in prophetic ecstasy on a Sunday (1:10). It is not meant for John personally, but for the entire Church, represented by the seven local churches of Asia Minor, since in the Bible seven is symbolic of completeness. The churches are addressed in order of the route John's message would travel (1:11). The account of John's vision is circulated to the churches so that it could be read aloud in the liturgical assembly (1:3), presumably on the Lord's day when the people of God gather for Eucharist. John's vision is also meant for the Church in every age and place, not just in the Roman world under Emperor Domitian.

A main theme in Revelation's inaugural vision (1:9–20) is that the exalted Christ stands among the churches. The vision is addressed to the seven selected local churches, with each one represented by a lamp (1:12, 20), though they clearly are a group that also symbolizes the universal Church. The exalted Christ, who is present in his people's midst, is depicted in this vision as king and priest. Revelation's ecclesiology is bound up with its Christology: in the seven letters Christ threatens to remove himself from the unfaithful churches, and promises to reward the faithful ones with his continued presence (2:5; 3:10–12). For John, the Church does not exist without the exalted Christ in her midst.

This introductory vision, like any inaugural vision of a great prophet (Isa 6), is a theophany, to which John responds as any Old Testament prophet would, namely, by falling in worship and holy fear. John's contemporary audience would thus immediately recognize him as a duly commissioned prophet in the line of the great prophets of the Old Testament, and it would likewise understand that Christ is equal to the God of the prophets. It is John's way of saying that Christ is equal in divinity to the Father. Moreover, in this vision, Christ is given the attributes and prerogatives of God found in the Old Testament (the Ancient of Days in Dan 7). It is comforting to the persecuted and culturally estranged churches of Asia Minor to know that Christ their God is present among them in their distress.

In John's inaugural vision, Christ is portrayed neither as the Lamb, nor as the earthly Christ of the Gospels, but as the risen and glorified Christ. It is Christ's triumph over suffering and death that is held up before the readers' eyes in order to assure them: he has the power to protect and help those who endeavor to endure faithfully. After Revelation finishes encouraging the Church, it closes with yet another vision of Christ Triumphant and enthroned in his people's midst (Rev 21—22).

The Son of Man figure in 1:13 serves to remind the reader that it is the suffering earthly Jesus now glorified who appears to John. The paradox that life is gained only through the cross of Christ is a predominant theme (5:9–10; 7:13; 12:10–11). The title "Son of Man" also reminds the original readers of the figure in Daniel 7 who receives from God the messianic kingdom. In Daniel 7 the kingdoms of this world give way to the kingdom given to the Son of Man (7:13–14, 23–27), which will endure forever. Christ is hereby portrayed as the Messianic King.

The use of the Old Testament here indicates that Christ is dressed in a priestly way as well ("a long robe"; see Ezek 9:2, 11; Dan 10:5–6), which highlights his exalted position and redemptive sacrifice, along with the royal priesthood of his people, in whose midst he stands (Rev 1:6, 9). As his Mystical Body shares in his kingship, so it does in his priesthood by embracing his redemptive sacrifice and death, by worshiping God alone, and by living in such a way that his presence remains in them. Thus Revelation's introduction and the seven letters to the churches are integrally related. In them we see Christ the Priest and his priestly people, Christ the King and his kingly reign among that people. This vision of Christ the King, exalted Son of Man, and Priest is intended to give courage to the kingdom of priests that serves him. It also serves to prepare the seven churches to heed what Christ says to them, because they have just been shown his true dignity and authority (2:1, 8, 12, 18; 3:1, 7, 14).

In his theophany, John sees Christ and not the Lord God (YHWH), yet uses titles reserved only for the Lord God (YHWH) in the Old Testament (see 1:17c and Isa 41:4; "the Living One" is a stock appellation for God in the Old Testament), as well as uses titles applied only to Christ (Rev 1:18b). This use of titles results in a confession of Christ's divinity and emphasizes that, like the Lord God, he lives eternally. He is distinct from the Father in that he "was dead," which is at the heart of Revelation's picture of Christ as the Lamb who was slain but now lives. The risen Christ is not separated by John from the suffering, dead, and buried Christ's person and work. Christ gives life because he is the "One Who Lives Forever" and has won the victory over death, thereby gaining the right and authority to hold the keys to death and Hades (a typical biblical pairing).

The sum of these titles is a description of Christ as the center of existence, displaying John's christocentric vision of reality. Christ is the "First and Last," in whom all things have their being and ultimate perfection; this is the vision of reality John has throughout the book, indicated by the framing of "First and Last" in 1:18 and 22:13. Revelation's eschatology is that Christ will bring all of creation to its ultimate goal. Christ will bring everything to its full consummation in himself, which has already begun with his incarnation, death, and resurrection. Thus Christ, the beginning and center of creation, is also its fulfillment. All things find their fulfillment in him because he is the "First and the Last, the Alpha and the Omega," the "One who was dead but lives forever." Fullness of life in Christ is the goal of all humanity. Christ saves because he is the principal of creation (3:14); only through him is it re-created and saved.

Questions

1. If this New Testament book is a "revelation," what does that mean exactly?
2. The author of this revelation claims to have visions. Does he really?
3. Who is the John who wrote this work?
4. Why does the first chapter have so many liturgical aspects to it?
5. Why is Christ described in this opening vision in such an unfamiliar way?
6. Why is witness or testimony to Christ so prevalent in this chapter? What does it mean and what is its relationship to "the word of God" also common here?

Conclusion

John's portrayal of Christ in this first section is significant; he is presented as the true king or imperator who is really in control, over against the Roman "king" (Domitian), who merely appears to be. Roman emperors were depicted on their coinage with the seven stars (i.e., the seven planets known at that time) in their right hand, representing their universal power. Christ is depicted here in the same way (1:16, 20) to convey that it is Christ who is truly king, and king of all the kings on earth (1:5; 17:17). He holds in his hand not only the universe, but the Church (1:20); he is the ground and center of all reality.

Christ is described as a king or emperor: he wears gold (the symbol of royalty) and white (the symbol of victory in conquering). In each letter Christ promises to reward those who share in his victory ("to everyone who conquers"; 2:7, 11, 17, 26; 3:5, 12, 21). The vision of Christ the Victorious King who now reigns is meant to encourage patient endurance in Jesus, so as to share in his kingship as his royal priestly people (1:5–6, 9; 5:9–10).

It is important to the persecuted communities to know this, because they are not free from the threat of imprisonment if they refuse to worship the Roman gods, including the emperor (13:7, 15). Christ stands in the midst of his Church as it battles and endures evil, and so reigns with him; the Mystical Body suffers and triumphs over evil with its Head. Christ promises protection from apostasy—not from physical death—and to give himself to all those who endure faithfully (2:10; 3:10). Sharing in Christ's victorious kingship means sharing in his cross even now, and it may also mean physical death. Similarly, Christ threatens to remove his presence from those who compromise with the prevailing idolatrous culture and deny him, or who do not remain in him.

Section Two:
Revelation 2:1—3:22

Introduction

Revelation's overall purpose is to encourage the Church's fidelity to Christ. For its author, John, this fidelity shows itself by the faithful "witness of Jesus," that is, in being willing to suffer for the sake of his word and truth, even unto death (12:11). Throughout the book, but especially in the seven letters of chapters 2 and 3, John exhorts the Church to be a people characterized by witness, charity, repentance, and faithful endurance (2:2–3, 4–5, 10, 13, 16; 3:2, 10; 14:12).

John sees the Church as the new people of God, with whom God has made a covenant in the blood of the "Lamb who was slain but now stands," Jesus Christ (1:5–6; 5:9–10). This covenanted people is a royal priesthood that reigns with Christ even now, since he is the exalted Son of Man present among the local churches faithful to him. John continually exhorts the Church to strive for holiness and charity lived in the truth of Christ (2:2–6; 3:1–3) because his vision of reality is one of God's glorious reign, already begun and enduring forever. For John, only the repentant and faithful will share eternally in Christ's triumph over death and in God's definitive defeat of evil by living in this kingdom, now as God's holy and covenanted children (2:5, 7, 10–11, 26–28; 3:12, 21). Accordingly, John's visions demonstrate how glorious and enduring is that reign of which the Church is a nascent expression, while at the same time showing everything not associated with Christ's truth to be putrid, horrid, and ultimately, a deadly lie.

The overall theme of the book is that God reigns, now and forever. Confident in this reality, John attempts throughout the book to encourage his fellow sufferers in the first-century churches of Asia Minor, beleaguered by hostile social and cultural environments as well as politically sponsored persecution, to view their situation in a positive way. John sees the entire cosmos not from the earthly perspective that despairs that evil still seems to be prince of this world, but from the heavenly one that proclaims that good reigns everywhere Christ's cross is embraced (1:5–9; 5:9–10). The paradox that real life is obtained only by embracing Christ's triumph over death on the cross undergirds this entire work; it is why the Lamb who was slain is the primary way of describing Christ in Revelation. John encourages his fellow sufferers to face the distress of evil and falsehood by patiently enduring in the crucified and risen Jesus, with whom they suffer and reign even now if they only live in faithful witness to him (1:9).

John continually tries to convey the profound notion that Christ's truth always brings opposition and suffering to those who are joined with it. Conversely, those who do not suffer for Christ's sake must repent of their complacency and compromising lifestyle. Those who do not suffer hardship for Christ's sake are therefore severely criticized for compromising the truth (2:14–16; 3:1–4, 15–19), while those who suffer faithfully for Christ are "rewarded" with more suffering (2:10; 3:10). Thus it follows logically for John that the Church can expect suffering as the inevitable result of a life faithful to Christ. What is good for the Master is good for the disciple; the one thing Christ promises in this world for those who follow him is persecution.

Questions

7. Why is there language of conquering and victory on Christ's lips in the seven letters?
8. What is to be made of some of the strange things mentioned in these letters: Nicolaitans, Balaam, Jezebel, Antipas, and even Satan's assembly and throne?
9. The saying "Let anyone who has an ear listen to what the Spirit is saying to the churches" occurs in all seven letters. What does it mean?

10. There appear to be so many specific details about daily life in these letters. How are these relevant to the rest of the book and to the later Church?

Conclusion

From the letters to the seven churches, we get a glimpse into the daily life of the Church in the eastern end of the Roman Empire at the end of the first century. As mentioned previously, the fact that there are seven letters is often taken to mean that they symbolize the universal Church throughout time and space. The letters are also universal in that they touch upon matters relevant to the Church in every age and place, including our own. For example, there is a call to repent for those who are unfaithful, and a call to be more faithful for those whose faith could be lived more fully. There is encouragement for those whose lives conform to Christ in suffering. Christ calls all his disciples to live in charity and truth, promising salvation to those who persevere in following him, even through hardship and persecution. There is a prophetic call for the Church to be countercultural.

John's ultimate concern is that Christians live the Gospel in an uncompromised fashion. Thus, through these seven letters, he exhorts his fellow Christians not to adopt or perpetuate those things in their contemporary culture that are contrary to the letter and spirit of the Gospel. John is given a prophet's task, namely, to write to each church whatever admonition and encouragement Christ gives him to deliver. John is also prophetic in criticizing the corruption and sinfulness of his society. The Church of the third millennium might not be faced with the same specific struggles as that of the first century, but it is still faced with the same discernment about what is good in the world and what is not conformable to life in Christ.

Review of Revelation 1—3

John relates the vision given to him as an early Christian prophet in exile for his faithful witness to Christ. His overall objective is to deliver God's word to his people so as to encourage the Church as it struggles against its persecutors. John crafts his apocalyptic–prophetic message within an epistolary framework. Both prophecy and letters are familiar in the biblical world; John is not devising something hitherto unknown. Neither is apocalyptic thinking unknown in the biblical world, even though there is comparatively little of it in the Bible. John's main point in the seven letters to the churches is that Christ is present in the midst of his faithful people. It is this Christ who appears in the opening vision as the risen, exalted, triumphant Son of Man, Almighty King of the Universe, and Lord of History. John's overall purpose, then, is to encourage and console his fellow sufferers in Christ.

This introductory section sets the stage for what comes next in the book. In chapters 4 and 5, John will be taken up into heaven to see God enthroned in his heavenly court together with visions that are designed to prepare and strengthen the faithful. There has not been very much by way of apocalyptic trappings so far; that will now change. If we remember that John says he was given this revelation of Jesus Christ by God so that he might show the faithful "what must soon take place" (1:1–2), we shall not lose our bearings: we can expect an unveiling about Jesus Christ to take place in this series of visions that follows the introductory one. The ultimate purpose of these visions is to make known to the Church of all times and places what is otherwise hidden about what must soon take place, that is to say, about the final consummation of the kingdom of God. Christ and his kingdom are the main subjects of this book, and that is nothing new to the Christian who is already familiar with the four Gospels.

REVELATION 4—5

Even a cursory glance at chapter 4 will tell the reader that a new major section of the book has begun. It is not always clear in a biblical text, especially in English translations, where the structural divisions lie. We forget the original autographs did not have the modern editorial niceties. Moreover, the Bible's chapters and verses are a medieval invention. Though they are convenient and conventional, they are sometimes not well placed (any knowledgeable reader of, say, Gen 1—11 knows this), both in terms of giving us direction or in accurately presenting the original author's structure of his own work.

The reason for determining a work's outline, and the original author's conception of it, is, of course, so that we can read the work aright. A biblical book's structure or outline properly orients the reader, like chapters and page numbers in a modern book. Getting the structure of a particular text right helps us to interpret that text in the way the original author intended, which is where all responsible interpretation of the biblical text must at least start. This is one reason why reading biblical texts apart from their proper contexts can lead to misinterpreting them. Naturally, it is impossible to determine the outline of a biblical book without reading it in the original. Good translations will, however, reflect and accurately represent those original texts, as the New Revised Standard Version of Revelation 4:1 does.

In any case, most biblical scholars agree that 4:1 begins a new section of the book. In fact, most also agree that 4:1 is the beginning of the major section of the book, so that 4:1—22:5 is usually identified as the "apocalypse proper." After reading chapters 1 to 3, that makes some sense; there is little strictly apocalyptic material there. If the reader looks at 22:6–21, it is fairly evident that the epistolary format found in chapter 1 is resumed. Thus, 22:6–21 is often understood to be the epistolary conclusion to the book.

However, within 4:1—22:5 there are further subdivisions. The difficulty is to discover what they are. It is often said that there are as many outlines of the book as there are heads that think about it. There do not appear to be clear enough indicators as to John's own detailed structure within this major apocalyptic section that forms the body of his work. He did, however, give some definite literary markers for its various subdivisions. In the course of this commentary, they will be pointed out. As for the overall structure, this commentator will follow a combination of what is generally recognized and her own discernment as to the original author's conception. The outline of 4:1—22:5 will be discussed as the commentary progresses, but for convenience and overview, it is presented here:

I. Chapters 4:1—22:5: Apocalyptic visions to prepare and strengthen the faithful for the consummation of the kingdom of God

   A An open door in heaven (4:1—11:18)
      1. God enthroned is worthy of worship (4:1—5:14)
      2. Septet of the seals (6:1—8:2)
      3. Septet of the trumpets (8:2—11:18)

   B The temple of God in heaven opens, ark of the covenant is seen (11:19—15:4)
      1. A great sign in heaven, and another sign (11:19—14:20)
      2. Another sign in heaven (15:1–4)

   B' The temple of the tent of witness in heaven opened (15:5—19:10)
      1. Septet of the bowls (15:5—16:21)
      2. "Babylon Appendix" (17:1—19:10)

   A' Heaven opened, the heavenly Rider-Warrior conquers (19:11—22:5)
      1. Victory of God's kingdom (19:11—20:15)
      2. God's covenantal dwelling with the faithful (21:1–8)
      3. "Jerusalem Appendix" (21:9—22:5)

Chapters 4 and 5 clearly belong together, which will be seen more easily once we get to chapter 6. These two chapters comprise the opening vision of the apocalypse proper. John is transported into heaven (4:1), where he sees God enthroned and the Lamb at his side. The heavenly court renders ceaseless praise to them. It may be helpful to approach reading chapter 4 together with chapter 5 if we think in terms of a camera filming the scene. Chapter 4 is the general panorama of heaven with all its inhabitants. Chapter 5 is the zoomed-in focus that gives us more detail, particularly of its center, the Lamb. Theological themes in this section will be treated in the material on each individual chapter and in their review.

Section Three:
Revelation 4:1–11

Introduction

After the inaugural vision and the letters to the seven churches, Revelation moves into the major part of the book. Revelation 4:1—22:5 contains a series of apocalyptic visions to prepare and strengthen the faithful in their struggles as they await the final consummation of the kingdom of God. Chapters 4 and 5 belong together as one vision, though for our purposes the two chapters can be treated successively.

Through an open door in heaven (4:1), certain secrets are unveiled to John. In essence, what John sees in this vision of 4:1—5:11 is God enthroned, reigning in his heavenly kingdom, with the heavenly court paying due homage and rendering loyal service. From this vision it is clear that the main image in the book is God and the Lamb enthroned.

It is only logical for the vision of God enthroned to be accompanied by a vision of his reign since they are two sides of the same coin, for one cannot have a kingdom without a king. So, at nearly every turn John relates a vision of either divine enthronement or God's reign. However, John's feet are firmly planted on the ground: God's Church on earth is in severe distress as it awaits the kingdom's final consummation with the necessary dual accompaniment of the ultimate destruction of evil and the fulfillment of all things in Christ. The Church, which gives visible earthly expression to God's incipient reign, suffers distress (12:10–17).

While John may tell the story from a heavenly perspective, he lives the reality of the persecuted Church on earth (1:9–10). For John, since hardship and suffering are the present lot of Christ's faithful, patient endurance is needed in order to reign with Christ on earth here and now, in faithful witness to him (1:9; 14:12). The life of the kingdom is possible here and now only by embracing the Paschal Mystery in one's own life. John intentionally refers to the Church as a kingdom (1:5–6). While this usage reflects an allusion to Exodus 19:6 and the covenant, it also serves to underscore the reality of the new people of God as subjects of the Messianic King. Thus we see that the visionary diptych of God enthroned and of his kingdom in chapters 4 and 5 also serves a specific practical purpose, namely, to encourage fidelity to Christ by the Church so that the royal people of God may continue to participate in his reign forever.

Christ is presented in this section as the Lamb "who was slaughtered but now stands," who shares God's throne. Christ, the first-born of the dead and ruler of kings on earth (1:5) is the faithful and true witness (1:5) to the reality of the cosmos: he is the divine principal of creation, salvation, and fulfillment. All things were created through him, and all things have their end in him: he is the Alpha and the Omega (1:5; 3:4; 12:10–11; 21:13). He sustains his Church, promising the reward of eternal life to his faithful people, which is expressed in various images (2:7, 10, 17, 26–28; 3:5, 12, 20–22).

In John's greeting to the Church in which he gives praise to Christ "who loves us" (1:4–6), the Church is called a kingdom of priests for God the Father (1:6), made so by Christ's love. The people of God have been freed from their sins by his blood (1:5). In Revelation, there is an important and intertwining connection between Christ, King and Priest, and the kingdom of priests he made in his blood. His priestly people owe God alone due worship. They belong to him with their identity rooted in service to him alone. (*Service* is a biblical word designating worship; see Joshua 24.)

Bound up with the image of God's enthronement, then, only God and the Lamb are deemed worthy of worship (7:15; 16:9; 15:4; 20:4). Idolatry, especially worship of "the Beast" or his prophet, is portrayed as a despicable deed that bars one from entry into the kingdom (13:8; 14:10–11; 19:20; 20:4; 22:15). Worshiping God alone is a prominent theme in Revelation, so much so that John's attempt to pay simple homage to an angel—yet without committing idolatry—is corrected twice (19:10; 22:9).

Typical of John's theological logic, the primary activity of those who reject Christ is idolatry. Repentance is always used in Revelation to mean either the abandonment of idolatry or the correction of abuse and complacency in worshiping God (2:20–23; 3:17–19; 9:20–21). Christ is worthy of worship because he is All in All, while the Beast is nothing. The Church is described as a royal, priestly people (1:6; 5:10; 20:6), an allusion to Exodus 19, which indicates that the Church is a people set apart for service to God, as the old people of God were. This "setting apart" has been sealed with the blood of the Lamb, making the Church his covenanted people. One of the Church's primary services on earth as this royal, priestly people is to worship Christ. For Revelation, life in Christ is all that ultimately matters, and this is expressed primarily in worship of and service to him.

Like the inaugural visions of Old Testament prophets, this is a vision of God enthroned in splendor and royal majesty, as God Almighty on his heavenly throne (e.g., Isa 6; Ezek 1—2). Although chapters 4 and 5 are not another inaugural vision, John wishes his readers to connect the opening vision of the exalted Christ (1:9–20) to this vision of God enthroned, so that the seven churches' relationship to Christ can be seen in the context of the whole of salvation history and not simply in their present and individual relationship to him. John understands the risen Christ to be enthroned now with God (11:15–17). Christ is the Lamb whose incarnation, death, and resurrection defeated Satan (chap. 12), and who alone has the right to carry out the divine plan of salvation (represented by the scroll of chap. 5—6). The verbal connections between 4:1–2 and 1:9–10 tie both visions together. Revelation 4:1 resumes the vision of the risen Christ from chapter one (1:19 and 4:1) in order to set the seven letters within their proper context: the seven local churches are to heed what the Spirit says in John's entire prophetic revelation and to see their particular situations within the entire scope of God's universal plan of salvation. The specific messages are to be heeded by each community, in part because they stand before God's throne with Christ in their midst, and in part because what is taking place "now and hereafter" (1:19;

4:1) is part of the divine economy for the universal Church and all humanity.

Questions

11. In the opening part of this chapter, the seer describes being transported to heaven, where he sees God. Can this really have happened? What does this mean theologically?
12. The description of God and his heavenly court is fantastic and confusing. Why is God described this way?
13. Who are the bizarre creatures described in this vision, and what is their purpose?

Conclusion

Though modern Western Christians tend not to think of God as king enthroned in heaven and served in a courtly fashion, it is a useful image, and very much in line with the thinking of the New Testament. To speak of God as king is to suggest that he rules with a providential care over the creation he made from nothing. It suggests, too, that he knows what he is about in exercising his supreme sovereignty over the universe. The image implies that he *has* a kingdom, something that Christians may easily take for granted, even though they pray daily to enter it ("Thy kingdom come"). Chapter 4 seeks to remind the Church that God reigns even now, and although there may be many who break the first commandment or who refuse even to acknowledge God's kingship, there are those already in heaven who render him ceaseless and due worship. Christians live in hope to join them one day in that kingdom that will never end. Jesus preached often about the kingdom of God and what it is like (e.g., Matt 13). John's vision elaborates on the kingdom material found in the Gospels. This vision in chapter 4 conveys the message that "God's will be done on earth as it is in heaven," that is, that God desires every creature on earth to render him ceaseless and due homage. That starts here and now and is to continue for all eternity.

Another benefit of this perhaps-unexpected depiction of God in chapter 4 is that it is filled with rich and varied symbols and images. John may be gazing into heaven, but if we close our eyes we may have a better grasp of the thrust of this passage: we might let the scene in all its multifacetedness make its impact on our imagination. What do the colors, the sounds, the smells, and the movements taken *as a whole* convey? It is significant that the major apocalyptic section of the book begins with *this* scene. The keynote to 4:1—22:5 that is sounded here is one of divine majesty, holy awe, perfect sovereignty, universal dominion, eternal glory, and providential care. It is, for the Christian persevering in the face of evil or persecution, a scene that conveys great hope, joy, and consolation. It is an encouragement to continue to be faithful temporally so as to enjoy eternally the victory promised by Christ in the letters of the previous chapters. It is a reminder that the admonitions, exhortations, and promises of those seven letters have a real orientation: life with our heavenly Father in his kingdom, where he lives and reigns forever, in complete peace, justice, and holiness.

God is praised in this scene mainly as the Almighty Creator who is holy and worthy of all worship. He is also described as he "who was and is and is to come" (4:8), an expression that is used frequently of God in this book (already in 1:8). This expression should make the reader sit up and take notice, for one expects "who was, is, and *will be*" rather than *"to come,"* if there is to be consistency in phrasing. The "who was and is" reminds us of Exodus 3 where God reveals himself to Moses as the great "I Am (Who Am)," that is, essentially as the God who exists, a living God who causes anything that exists to be. So why should John not be consistent in phrasing? John wants to highlight the fact that he and other Christians are expecting God to come again, in his Anointed One. John and the early Church believed intensely in a Second Advent of Christ in glory. Part of the end-time (eschatological) outlook of this book is expressed in this divine appellation. There will be more discussion of the eschatological outlook of this book later.

Section Four: Revelation 5:1–14

Introduction

This section is part of a twofold vision of God and the Lamb enthroned that starts at 4:1, the beginning of the book's major apocalyptic section, which stretches to 22:5. As we pick up Revelation's narrative at 5:1–5, only the Lamb "who was slaughtered" comes forward from God enthroned to receive the scroll, for he alone is worthy to open it. He is first described and shown to be worshiped by the heavenly assembly (5:6–8), and then a hymn is sung to him (5:9–10), which tells of his redemptive death and its result, namely, the creation of a royal, priestly people to serve God and reign with him forever (5:9–10). This communion between God and humanity is the ultimate purpose of creation, as demonstrated in the eschatological vision (21:1—22:5) and foreshadowed here. As the vision continues, John focuses on the voices of myriads of angels and of the assembly that surrounds the throne, which includes the twenty-four elders and the four "living creatures," who cry out in praise of the Lamb's worthiness to break open the seals. He alone can carry out the divine plan of salvation and bring the kingdom of God to its consummation. The Lamb alone is worthy because of his sacrificial death and resurrection. John's soteriology and eschatology are intertwined.

Revelation's central theme of the consummation of God's kingdom is shown here in a vision of God enthroned with the Lamb. This vision enjoys a primacy of place in the apocalyptic visions of Revelation; it precedes all the septets and the eschatological events. The establishment of God's reign entails the rooting out of evil, which in turn involves bringing sinners to repentance. This is the train of the narrative from here until the end of the book. The

Lamb is depicted as enthroned with the Father, and receiving ever-lasting dominion. Christ reigns by virtue of the cross and resurrection, hence the Lamb "standing as if it had been slaughtered" is an apt image (and very biblical) for emphasizing his unique sacrifice. This is another fine example of Revelation's use of covenant-exodus imagery and of rereading the Old Testament in the light of Christ. The sevenfold worthiness sung in 5:12 indicates the Lamb's full kingship and authority, divinely conferred. Since God alone is Creator, King, and Redeemer, he alone is worthy of worship. His almightiness is a reflection of his power to rule the universe and to save the creation he has made.

John's theology that God alone is worthy of worship comes to the fore here; it is the major theme of chapters 4 and 5. By all aspects of creation God is worshiped: angels, animals, nature, and humanity are all represented by the various members of the heavenly court. In 5:14 the four "living creatures" represent the natural world, which gives praise to God unceasingly. The twenty-four elders also worship God and the Lamb continually (4:4–8). They worship God by falling in homage. Because they acknowledge his kingship by casting aside their own crowns, they represent redeemed humanity, which ought always to recognize God's providential sovereignty over all mankind. In addition, the elders play harps and hold gold vessels, which are the prayers of the saints (5:8), an indication that they are priests (the Greek word here is *presbyter*, translated either as "elder" or "priest"), offering due sacrifice to God on behalf of all humanity. The whole universe (note the threefold cosmology in 5:13) is to give full homage to the Lamb (5:12) and to God (5:13). The assembly answers "Amen" to affirm that universal worship—from the natural and supernatural orders—of God is fitting. This vision assures the persecuted and beleaguered Church on earth that it is not alone in such worship, but joins a larger community.

Questions

14. What is the mysterious scroll that is given to the Lamb and why must someone be worthy to open it?

15. Why should Christ be symbolized as a Lamb that "was slaughtered"? Who, then, is the Lion of the tribe of Judah and the Root of David?
16. In addition to the seven eyes and seven horns of the Lamb, there are also seven seals on the scroll. What is the significance of seven here?
17. The four "living creatures" and the twenty-four elders sing a new hymn: Why? And what is its significance?

Conclusion

Revelation's theology underscores the paradox that true life only comes from Christ's triumphant death on the cross, a viewpoint also found in the Gospel of John. John sees the Church as the suffering Body of Christ, and like its Head who reigns from the cross, so the Church shares, even now, in the triumphant reign of the Lamb who was slaughtered but now lives. What really matters to John is how the people of God respond to hardship and evil that come to them for Christ's sake. He knows that those who worship and follow the Lamb share in his reign even now on earth as his priestly people (5:9–10). He likewise knows that those who compromise and follow the deceitful ways of the Beast on earth, although they are given plenty of opportunity and divine encouragement to repent, will not enter the kingdom of God. Those who have preferred citizenship in the vile and idolatrous Babylon are not fit for the splendor and purity of the heavenly Jerusalem.

Revelation, then, primarily serves to exhort the faithful people of God to remain faithful, by relating visions of Christ, God, and his kingdom, and by showing in a fantastic and highly symbolic way that worshipers of the Beast really are lovers of falsehood and, conversely, lovers of falsehood really are in league with Satan (22:15); they have rejected the offer of divine patience and chastisement meant to bring them to repentance. To drive the point home and encourage fidelity to Christ, Revelation presents the believer with visions of saints and the members of the heavenly court already enjoying eternal life and sharing in Christ's reign (especially chap. 7).

In Revelation the Church is a new royal, priestly people whose nature is marked by service and worship of the Lamb. There is a good deal of covenant-exodus imagery in Revelation. We see it, for example, in the septets in John's rereading of the Egyptian plagues, but also in other key places, such as 1:5–6, 12; 5:6; 11:18–19; 12:14; 15:5; and 21:1–5. God made himself a new people by a new exodus and saved them with a new covenant in the blood of the Lamb (1:5–6; 5:9–10). The implication of John's reworked covenant-exodus imagery is that just as God re-creates in Christ, so he liberates his new people (who are a new Israel) with a new covenant-exodus in Christ. The result is that the Church's purpose is to serve and worship God as a priestly people that keeps this new covenant (12:17; 19:8). Like the Mosaic covenant, the covenant of the Lamb is made with a people, not with individual persons. That is why in Revelation, worship, especially in heaven, is always communal. God's new priestly nation is a people set apart, not a group of individuals. This is especially clear in the book's opening doxology, which declares that Christ has loved us, and freed us from our sins, and made us a kingdom, priests for God (1:5–6).

In Revelation service and worship of the Lamb is what identifies those who follow him as his people. It is the primary activity of the covenanted priestly people. For John, worship of God is what being a priestly people involves; it is what they are set apart to do and what in this life they prepare to do forever. In 4:1—22:5, whenever the Lamb stands in the midst of his faithful people (7:13–17; 14:1–5), they are always shown in adoration of him. God's priestly people, covenanted to him, cannot worship the Beast because, for John, worship is formative and expressive of the followers of the Lamb. In Revelation, citizenship in one city or the other is shown by worship: either one is a citizen of the Bride or of the Harlot (addressed later). These two kingdoms represent two opposed loyalties, which are shown by whom they worship. The entire book is set within a liturgical context (1:3, 4–8; 22:12–21), and there are many scenes of liturgical worship and hymns in order to encourage the new priestly people on earth to be faithful as a royal people that was formed and called to worship and serve God alone.

For John, what characterizes the new people of God, therefore, both here and beyond, is service and worship as a royal people. Worship is salvation and citizenship in the heavenly Jerusalem. Thus, those who worship the Beast do not gain entry. Since membership in the heavenly Jerusalem is determined by citizenship and worship in this life, those who refuse due adoration of the Lamb in this life, thereby preferring citizenship in Babylon, cannot be part of the priestly people covenanted to him in the kingdom (chap. 21—22).

In Revelation, the Church's witness of Jesus and worship of the Lamb are intimately linked: the Mystical Body that bears Jesus' own presence is the priestly people covenanted in his blood, who were brought out of a spiritual Egypt to serve God as his royal priesthood. The Church's role and nature are inseparable. Both her witness and worship contribute to and participate in Christ's work of salvation.

Review of Revelation 4—5

Chapters 4 and 5 are certainly meant to be read together as a unit. The scene that opens with John's being transported to heaven is clearly continued by the action of the Lamb receiving the scroll from God. Chapters 4 and 5 follow on the divine directive that the seer is to write down in a book "what you see and send it to the seven churches" (1:3, 11, 19). The first thing John relates to the churches is his inaugural vision and the seven letters to them (1:12—3:22). Since the revelation continues with the new series of visions begun at 4:1, he then relates that to them. The inaugural vision and the seven letters are introductory; the vision of 4:1—5:14 begins the main apocalyptic portion of the book.

Many people find it hard to identify the themes in this book. The theological themes are very much connected to the book's literary design and its original historical-political context. The theological theme of the new covenant made in the blood of the Lamb is discernible in the book's use of exodus imagery and language. The theme of God's providential care over all creation is found in the words of the hymns sung in his praise. That God alone is worthy of worship is a theme perhaps readily recognized, and the original context of Christians being persecuted for refusing to worship the Roman emperor helps us see that.

Revelation's themes, imagery, and language are deeply rooted in the Old Testament, so that the better one knows the Old Testament, the easier it is to understand this book. If John can employ new exodus and covenant imagery, it is because he rereads the Old Testament in light of what God has done in Christ. A major key to understanding the book, therefore, is its use of the Old Testament. John has created a masterpiece of intricately woven allusions to the Old Testament, a veritable tapestry that retells the story of salvation in light of the "Christ event." We have already seen this, for example, in the inaugural vision in chapter 1, where the exalted Christ is described in terms used of

God himself in the Old Testament, and in the description of God enthroned in chapter 4. Many Old Testament titles of God are used with Christ, and allusions to the exodus and creation stories, as well as to the great prophets, are especially significant for understanding Revelation's theology.

One of the book's predominant themes is at the fore in this first section of the "apocalyptic portion" of the book: God alone is worthy of worship. God wills the salvation of all humanity. For John, to be saved means to participate eternally in the kingdom of God, where he is perpetually worshiped. The purpose of all creation is to worship God, beginning in this created world and continuing into the re-created one hereafter. In this life, the people of God who are part of the new covenant of the Lamb must worship God, and the unfaithful must take it up. Worship is an important theme in Revelation by which John expresses the nature of the kingdom of God and the goal toward which all the cosmos moves. It is this theme that will especially help put the rest of the "apocalyptic portion" of the book in perspective.

REVELATION 6:1—8:2

The vision of the seven seals with the four horsemen is probably the best-known portion of Revelation. After having witnessed the Lamb receive the scroll with its seven seals, John is now shown what the scroll contains.

With the opening of the first seal of the scroll given to the Lamb, who alone is worthy to open it (6:1), John relates a series of visions that depict God's plan of salvation in Christ. There is a shift of emphasis from the previous chapters. The main focus is now on the defeat of evil, the soteriological reason for the incarnation, and the consequent distress experienced by humanity in this great cosmological battle. The series of septets in chapters 6 to 20 illustrates what awaits those who refuse to worship God and prefer to conform to the world and to worship idols. If the godly suffer because God allows it so that they may be conformed to Christ, the ungodly suffer divine punishments with the end of chastising sinners so as to move them to repentance, in the hope of their salvation.

The first four seals (the four horsemen; 6:1–8) form a unit, depicting wars and natural disasters that are naturally part of a fallen world. Thus these four seals are simultaneous, describing various aspects of the reality human beings find themselves in as a result of the Fall. The four "living creatures" cry out for each horseman to come forth to show the power over history and nature that the Lamb has. The horsemen have been given authority by God to kill one quarter of the earth, which includes the godly and ungodly unlike. These seals tell the story of the world as it currently is; no group of people (godly or ungodly) is singled out. The one quarter that is killed indicates that evil is limited by the permissive control of God and that there is still time to repent because the end of the world has not yet come.

In the fifth seal (6:9–11), the souls of the martyrs under the altar in heaven cry out for justice (6:10). The point here is that God's truth and holiness demand that innocent blood be avenged. But each martyr is given a long white robe (an image of victory and salvation; see chap. 2—3) and told to "rest a little longer, until the number would be complete both of their fellow servants and of their brothers and sisters, who were soon to be killed as they themselves had been killed" (6:11). It is not that God delights in human suffering, but that in his mysterious plan of salvation the end of evil somehow involves it. Put another way, divine mercy means that God awaits the repentance of all. Such forbearance, however, inevitably results in more suffering and even martyrdom of the faithful because they reign with Christ even now by participating in his redemptive mission in this world (1:9; 5:10).

The justice of God also requires judging the martyrs' cause among the "inhabitants of the earth" (6:10), a phrase always pejorative in the book. This important phrase refers to a group of people who are hostile to God and his Church. These people are never said to repent; in fact they just become increasingly hard of heart. The whole scene of the fifth seal conveys to the Church that God does not turn a blind eye to justice or to the evil perpetrated on the faithful. Since the entire struggle between good and evil is in his hands, the Church can live in hope.

The sixth seal (6:12–17) is a depiction of the distress involved in the final defeat of evil. Such immediate succession of judgment (sixth seal) on the heels of the cry for justice (fifth seal) indicates God's fidelity in answering the martyrs' cry. Their prayers are efficacious, and apparently connected causally to the sixth seal: the suffering and prayer of the faithful help to overcome evil; their suffering is salvific.

The seventh seal is not found until 8:1–5, after an extended "intermission" in chapter 7. Before the seventh seal there is a bipartite expansion, 7:1–8 and 7:9–17. In the first part of the chapter, the faithful are sealed on their foreheads. God does not allow the angels of 7:1–2 to do harm until his servants are sealed.

The 144,000 symbolize the true Israel, the Church. The sealing is another proof of God's fidelity; not only does he answer the cry for justice, he also protects the just when he renders it. Revelation 7:1–17 is in direct relationship to the sixth deal, which depicts the great and final tribulation. In 7:1–8, the faithful are prepared for and preserved from the distress that the sixth seal brings. In the second part of the chapter (7:9–17), there is a vision of all the elect (the "great multitude" of 7:9), which consists of not just the true Israel that has survived the great tribulation, but also those ungodly who repent as a result of it, as 7:13–14 indicates. This is an image of universal salvation. Redemption of all peoples is by the Lamb and his blood (7:14). Fidelity to God in worship is rewarded (7:15) with the fullness of his kingdom (7:16–17) and absence of distress.

The seventh seal (8:1) seems odd at first, not least of all because it is so brief. The heavenly silence gives a dramatic effect, and indicates the presence of God, as in the Old Testament (Zeph 1:7 and Zech 2:13). In the Book of Revelation heaven is never mentioned without a corresponding liturgy, because in heaven God is continually worshiped. The context would suggest, then, that the silence is not to allow the prayers of the martyrs to be heard, because they have already been answered, but because now is the time for a liturgical silence to celebrate the dwelling of God with his people, or at least to symbolize the patient hope of his coming. The silence is also a way of describing that the labors of the faithful are at an end. The silence here would indicate a sabbath rest, both for God and humanity. The final distress is characterized in Revelation by a great cosmic upheaval, in a way antithetical to its creation. John envisions that the consummation of all things, including salvation history, will be a re-creation. Creation must undergo a reversion to chaos (Gen 1) in order to be rid of evil (Gen 6—9). It is not wiped out, but re-created by God out of the upheaval.

Section Five: Revelation 6:1–17

Introduction

The septets of the seals (6:1—8:2), trumpets (8:2—11:19), and bowls (15:1—16:21) place the distress of the Church in this age within the context of life in Christ: with the incarnation the cosmic battle between good and evil, by which the kingdom is consummated, is intensified. Apparently, God allows the faithful to undergo the onslaught of evil, permitting them to be tested (2:10; 3:10) so as to make them worthy of the kingdom and to complete, however mysteriously, his plan of salvation (6:10). He allows the unfaithful to suffer in order to test them as well (3:10) and to exact justice for their hostility to him and his people. The visions of chapters 4 and 5, which follow immediately after the letters to the churches, portray God and the Lamb enthroned, and the worship given them conveys God's holiness and power. These images provide the essential key to understanding the relationship of chapters 1 to 5, to 6 to 20: the destruction of evil depicted in 6 to 20 is demanded by God's holiness and carried out by his power and his will (direct or permissive). In one sense, chapters 4 and 5 encourage the faithful in a positive way, whereas chapters 6 to 20 exhort by the negative means of violent visions of destruction and trial. The preservation of the faithful, a recurring motif in chapters 6 to 20, is a proof of God's justice. Another positive aspect for the faithful who suffer tribulation described in 6 to 20 is the salvific intervention of God. In rooting out evil, God manifests fidelity to his promise of salvation: his kingdom will be consummated when evil is finally destroyed.

Questions

18. The Book of Revelation extensively uses symbols and images. What is the best way to approach these symbols? Why did John not write plainly and simply instead of in a covert code?
19. What can be said about the one-quarter destruction of the earth?
20. Do the seven seals describe the end of the world? Are they therefore a blueprint for the future of humanity? Will the end of the world happen exactly (literally) like this, with the sun turning black and the moon into blood?
21. The seven seals seem to be more the work of an angry god rather than of Jesus Christ (the Lamb); why are they so violent and apparently vindictive?

Conclusion

Chapters 4 and 5 help put 6 in perspective. Because humanity has from the beginning refused to give due homage to its Creator, it has brought disaster upon itself and now finds itself in constant strife and hardship. However, God in his mercy limits the evil that humanity perpetrates and does not allow sin and death to be the ultimate definition of the creature made in his image (see Gen 3). God is just and merciful, holy and true, Master and Judge. He is Creator and Lord of History. Humanity must in the end face its maker and account to God.

If the six seals in chapter 6 present us with a picture of the world since the Fall, they do so in imagery and symbol. These seals, then, simply tell the story of the effect of original sin in the world. With sin comes evil and death. Disobedience to God brings alienation from other human beings. And so, strife, bloodshed, inhumanity, and injustice—all at the hands of human beings—are the result of the Fall. Nature too has suffered corruption as a result of humanity's Fall, and so natural disasters are also part of the fallen world in which we live. What John has told by the first six seals is virtually the same story that is told in a mythological way in Genesis 3 to 11: strife, bloodshed, inhumanity, and injustice (the first four seals) are all present there. (This interpretation comes from *The Apocalypse,* by Corsini. See the bibliography.) Like the fifth seal, the cry for God's vengeance on innocent shed blood is also seen in Genesis. The unjust hate the just so much as to murder them. In the fifth seal, the martyrs are slaughtered for their witness to the word of God. They are all those who were slain for keeping the covenant, old or new (and so Old Testament saints and Christians alike). The sixth seal has its parallel in Genesis 3 to 11 in the idea that the sinner wishes to hide from God and his just anger, as Adam and Eve did.

As a result of the Fall, all humanity now faces divine judgment. The sixth seal does not reveal who or what can save us, and then the opening of the final seal is delayed. However, we already know the answer. John told us in chapter 5 that the Lamb alone is worthy to open the scroll. The weeping of John there demonstrates his and God's desire for humanity's salvation. The sixth seal reiterates that desire, expressed in the language and imagery of the Old Testament prophets. We can expect, therefore, that the incarnation, death, and resurrection of the Son of God will save humanity, enabling it to withstand God's just judgment (6:17) and to enter the kingdom of God.

Section Six:
Revelation 7:1—8:2

Introduction

Chapter 7 interrupts the opening of the seven seals. Just as we expect the breaking open of the seventh seal, John "pauses." The seventh seal is not opened until 8:1. But it is necessary to study 7:1–17 to understand its place in the seals. The "pause," which most Revelation scholars refer to as an interlude, will help us interpret the material at hand, the septet of the seals.

The interlude of 7:1–17 falls between the sixth (6:12–17) and seventh seals (8:1–2). There are two sections to this interlude, marked off clearly by John's usual "then I saw" comment that indicates a new vision (or a new part of a one; see 5:1, 6). What John sees in this twofold vision of chapter 7 is the faithful redeemed of humanity, the "servants of God," sharing in God's heavenly reign. They join the rest of the heavenly court in perpetual worship of God and the Lamb. They praise God particularly in terms relevant to them, that is, for salvation (7:10), a word rarely used in this book and therefore all the more significant when it appears. John is told by one of the elders, who interprets the scene for him, that these saints are those who have "come out of the great ordeal; they have washed their robes and made them white in the blood of the Lamb" (7:14). These are the ones who have withstood the ordeal of the sixth seal by accepting and persevering in salvation by the blood of the Lamb.

Thus this interlude seems to be intended as a concrete answer to the question posed in 6:17: "Who can stand?" John's answer, directly dependent on the Old Testament prophet Joel, is that "the faithful can stand" because they are washed in the blood of the Lamb and have borne faithful witness to him. This vision of the salvation of the faithful—in which there is no more pain, weeping, hunger, or thirst, and where the redeemed enjoy being members of the flock of the Lamb—encourages the Church as it struggles in the world and endures persecution. God protects those who pay him due homage, worshiping him alone (7:1–3), and eventually brings them to eternal salvation where they will enjoy perpetual worship of him in his kingdom (7:15). This scene of the elect enjoying eternal bliss is a welcome relief to the violence, distress, and upheaval of the previous six seals.

In 8:1–2, John returns to the septet of the seven seals. The seventh seal is short and curious: it brings silence in heaven for half an hour. For this short period, there is an absence of movement, sound, and deed, seemingly even of the divine praises by the heavenly court. The next septet is connected to this seal when John sees the seven angels who hold the seven trumpets.

Questions

22. Who are the 144,000 who have been sealed? Are they related to the great multitude in 7:9?
23. What is the effect on the reader of the delay in opening the seventh seal?
24. What is the meaning of the silence in heaven for half an hour?

Conclusion

The interlude that is 7:1–17 clearly helps illuminate the first six seals and prepares the reader for the seventh. We are accustomed to thinking that everything in Revelation describes the end of the world, but that is not so. As with other books in the Bible, the end must be seen in light of the beginning and the ultimate purpose of creation, especially the creation of humanity. That is what John has done in the seven seals. The first five seals tell us why someone is needed to fulfill God's plan of salvation at all. The

Lamb is needed to redeem fallen humanity. All humanity will be judged by God (sixth seal), but only the faithful will come through the ordeal, with God's mercy (7:1–3), and enter into the kingdom of God. Having washed their robes and made them white in the blood of the Lamb (7:14), they will share in his victory over sin and death, after having withstood his just judgment (sixth seal).

Salvation is the ultimate goal toward which humanity's history tends. Often in apocalyptic thinking, the history of the world is divided into seven ages, the last being a sabbath. John may envision his seven seals as expressing the history of the world, with the seventh seal and its rest as a "sabbath age." As in Genesis 1, there are six days in which there is speaking and movement. On the seventh day God rests, and so there is silence: no speaking and no movement. The world and history will end, and that end is like the beginning, containing a sabbath. There will be no more toil, but only worship of God (which in Genesis is what the sabbath is for). John sees humanity's ultimate end in terms of a new creation that culminates in a sabbath in which the salvation and victory won by the Lamb will be celebrated by the worship of the triune God by his faithful servants. The history of humanity (seals one through five) does not end in the judgment of God (seal six) but in his merciful salvation (seal seven). Humanity's destiny is in the hands of the Lamb (who opens all the seals), who alone is worthy to carry out God's plan of salvation.

The silence in heaven is an echo from Zechariah 2, where the prophecy of a new Jerusalem is proclaimed to the Jewish exiles recently returned from Babylon. There, God's people are told to flee from daughter Babylon (Zech 2:6–13). The Lord announces impending judgment on Babylon for her mistreatment of his beloved people. He then announces he is coming to Jerusalem, to dwell among his people once again (Zech 2:14). Of particular note is God's advent, the result of which is, on the one hand, judgment on the enemies of his people, and, on the other, salvation for his people: he will dwell with them once again. The "nations" will also be brought into the worship of the Lord (Zech 2:15). Finally, the prophet commands, "Be silent, all people, before the Lord; for he has roused himself from his holy

51

dwelling" (Zech 2:13). This text and its prophecy seem to be the background for the seventh seal and also for the trumpets; this latter point will be discussed below.

There is also another Old Testament prophetic text that is alluded to here in the mention of silence, Zephaniah 1:7: "Be silent before the Lord GOD! For the day of the LORD is at hand." The wider context of this verse is that the Lord will judge his people for their idolatry and for their not serving him alone. This day of the Lord is a day of wrath, distress, and ruin (Zeph 1:14), on which the trumpet blast will be heard. This ominous warning is echoed by John in the silence that precedes the blasts of the seven trumpets. It is a warning for God's people to return to the true worship of the Lord and to forsake idolatry and all compromises with the culture.

Review of
Revelation 6:1—8:2

In the septet of the seven seals, there are several major themes typical of the book that come to the fore. The theme of redemption by the blood of the Lamb is predominant throughout, from the opening of the first seal in 6:1 to the vision of the kingdom of God in 7:17 (notice the mixed metaphor of the Lamb as Shepherd). The consummation of the kingdom of God, with salvation for the faithful, is also a key theme here, put in terms of a new exodus and restoration to the new promised land (not on this earth). Salvation is universal, too, not just for one (ethnic) group. One of the book's favorite themes, that God's providence rules the cosmos, is also clearly in evidence here; he limits evil, saves the just, and patiently awaits the conversion of his enemies. The cosmic battle between good and evil is put within this context. The theme of humanity's Fall and re-creation is also present in this section. Really what we have here in this septet, then, is nothing unfamiliar, just the usual biblical themes but in an apocalyptic garb.

Though we might expect that the seven seals are all about the end of the world, each of them is not explicitly about that. Their overall orientation, however, is to the perfection of all things in Christ in the ultimate consummation of the kingdom of God and the final defeat of evil. To this end does John relate all his visions. John's purpose is to remind oppressed and beleaguered Christians that their real homeland is heaven, not any human empire or city. A new exodus in the Lamb will liberate them from evil in this present corrupt age and bring them home at last. The book really is all about the ultimate Christian hope, not divinely driven doom and disaster deservedly (or not) carried out on the ungodly.

In the septet of the seven seals, we saw that there was a pattern: the four horsemen, then two more seals, then an interlude, finishing with the seventh seal. This pattern will be repeated in the next septet. For now, we can simply conclude by reviewing how the seals fit together. The first six tell of the present state of humanity, the result of the Fall, and the just judgment of God. The interlude of chapter 7 provides hope for the salvation of all humanity by the Lamb who is worthy to save. The seventh seal fits perfectly with the first six and the interlude: the heavenly sabbath of the new creation is what awaits the just (their longings will be fulfilled at last; see 6:10). This interlude, therefore, nicely links the first six seals with the seventh by providing the portrayal of salvation that is God's desire for humanity from the beginning. It also helps prepare the reader for properly understanding the seventh seal's content.

REVELATION
8:2—11:18

The same pattern of the seals is now repeated in the seven trumpets (8:2—11:18), but the story is narrated in an intensified way, more fully described. That is to say, the same story of distress and the coming of the kingdom is being retold, but with a slightly different emphasis. In other words, the trumpets express another aspect of the same realities as were told in the seals. Recapitulation is one of the literary techniques the book uses for emphasis, thereby elaborating what has just been told, which is a good teaching technique. The recapitulation does not always follow the exact same pattern; changes serve to underscore important points and theology, sometimes highlighting a particular new thing so as to bring it into sharper focus. The pattern of the seven trumpets, like that of the seven seals, begins with four items of the septet evidently grouped together and set off from the last three. There is also an interlude, which, like that of the seals, is placed between the sixth and seventh items of the septet. As with the seals, there is an introduction to the trumpets (8:2–5). Revelation 8:2 indicates that the distress of this septet is also at God's hands. There is an overlap of the seals and trumpets at 8:2; this verse serves as a literary hinge connecting the two. The theological connection made thereby will be discussed below.

The first four trumpets (8:6–12), like the first four seals, concern the whole cosmos, but in this case one third of the cosmos, not one fourth. The Fall of creation is brought out more fully by this slight change of the pattern. This change increases the narrative tension and indicates that the faithful have been awaiting justice, it seems, since the beginning of humanity and in the face of increasing evil. The reader has been told justice will come to pass

(8:3–5), but has to wait out the first four trumpets before seeing its execution depicted, in the same way justice is "delayed" in the seals (the martyrs of the fifth seal are told to wait, and only after the sixth seal do we see they are rewarded). The delay between the assurance of justice's satisfaction in 8:3–5 and its actual depiction in the three woes (last three trumpets) is designed to highlight the patience and mercy of God toward unrepentant sinners as he, with great forbearance, awaits their conversion.

The three woes (the three last trumpets, 8:13—11:18), being the full-blown picture of assured justice (8:5), are divine chastisements on the inhabitants of the earth (8:13) that express the horror of unrepentance and the absolute futility of worshiping idols (9:20–21). They are chastisements, not punishments, because their purpose is to bring the unfaithful to repentance. If the pattern of the seals is recapitulated in the seven trumpets, with slight alterations for reasons of focus and intensity, then it would follow that the three woes are likewise a fuller elaboration of the realities already described in the seals.

As with the seven seals, after the sixth trumpet there is a twofold interlude (10 and 11:1–13). Chapter 10 is a vision of an angel from heaven who orders the revelation to be sealed up and commands John not to write it down "because there will be no more delay" (10:5–6). The situation is urgent (especially since it follows immediately on 9:20–21): the wicked need to repent now and the just must remain faithful. The theme of delay in the seals is repeated in the interlude of the trumpets but intensified so as to underscore the urgency of repentance. In the interlude of the seals there is a delay so that the just can be preserved (7:3–4, by sealing). Now, in the interlude of the trumpets, there is no need for more time for the Church's preparation and preservation, for that has already been given. Chapter 11 in an allegorical way describes the role of the just in bringing the unrepentant to repentance.

Revelation 10:7 defines the seventh trumpet as the fulfillment of the mystery of God (announced to his servants the prophets; see 1:3). Although the seventh trumpet is also the third woe (10:7; 11:14–19), it describes the final triumph (as does the seventh seal) of the kingdom. Instead of silently worshiping in God's presence, the elect sing hymns of praise (11:15–17). The seventh trumpet is an expanded description of the seventh seal, while at the same time describing only the beginning of the kingdom's consummation, the completion of which—together with the description of the final defeat of evil—will be told later in the book. In the seventh trumpet the Lord has come to dwell among his people as prophesied: notice there is no "who is to come" in 11:17; the usual third element of the expression is dropped because he has begun his reign by coming to Jerusalem to dwell among his people once again. God's advent results in judgment on his enemies and salvation for his people, as prophesied in Zechariah 2 (and other places) and echoed in the seventh seal. Notice, then, how the seventh seal and the seventh trumpet are similar, but the seventh trumpet fleshes out the seventh seal. Notice, too, how both of the seventh items in the septet exclusively describe triumph and salvation, only implying judgment but not depicting it, so as to emphasize the ultimate hope of God's people. There is no hint of vindictiveness against enemies or persecutors. One can see that Revelation, in the end, brings not doom and damnation, but rather hope and salvation.

Section Seven:
Revelation 8:2—9:20

Introduction

The septet of the trumpets follows that of the seals and is intimately connected to it. This can easily be seen not only by the interrelation of 8:1 and 8:2 but by a simple list of the trumpets and their contents:

First trumpet: Land and vegetation devastated
Second trumpet: Sea devastated
Third trumpet: Fresh water devastated
Fourth trumpet: Celestial lights devastated
Fifth trumpet/first woe: Fallen star and locust army from
    the abyss
Sixth trumpet/second woe: Four angels on river's banks
    and demonic horses
                Interlude of Revelation 10—11
Seventh trumpet/third woe: No more delay but fulfillment
    of God's plan; kingdom consummated (11:15–18)

The trumpets are meant to recall the plagues of the exodus story unleashed against the Egyptians, so they would let God's people go. The first trumpet is like the seventh plague against Egypt (Exod 9:23); the second and third trumpets are like the first plague (Exod 7:20); and the fifth trumpet/first woe combines elements from the eighth and ninth plagues (Exod 10). The woes are directed against the inhabitants of the earth, that is, against the enemies of God and his people. They are chastisements meant to bring repentance, especially to turn people from idols to the worship of the only living and true God. Thus, the first four trumpets are natural devastations, permitted by God, and the fifth and sixth are supernatural and demonic, also within the divine will. The first four are not directed at anyone in particular, whereas the last three woes are. This is in part what makes the last three trumpets woeful. God's faithful are preserved (Rev 9:4) throughout these plagues, as in the exodus story (and 3:10). Revelation 8:3–5, in which prayers of the saints go up to heaven, indicates that God hears the cry of the just. Also, like the fifth seal, vengeance is for God to render against the enemies of his people. The seventh trumpet/third woe is twofold: it is the victory of God and his Messiah, together with the consummation of the kingdom, as well as being the final destruction of evildoers.

Revelation 8:2 concludes the seals and commences the trumpets. This literary overlapping signals a theological interrelation as well. Like the seals, the trumpets' narrative is the story of the state of humanity since the Fall. In the seals, the focus is on humanity's sinfulness, inhumanity, and injustice, and thus justifies God's wrath. There is also included, however, the theme of salvation for the faithful. In the trumpets, the recapitulation, which we recognize because of the similar pattern, shifts the focus slightly to the fall of the rest of creation. The first four trumpets describe the fall of nature (earth, water, sky) and its devastating effects on humanity. The fifth and sixth describe the Fall of the angels and, similarly, its devastating effects on humanity. Thus, in the trumpets we have a continuation of the seals in the story of the Fall (a "recapitulation"), with a filling-out of the story, resulting in a progression in the recapitulation. This is an old familiar biblical story retold here: with the Fall of humanity, the rest of creation is harmed and corrupted. The Fall results in devastation of humanity on humanity (e.g., Adam against Eve, Cain against Abel, etc.) as well as on all of the cosmos, which in turn causes more devastation.

Questions

25. Who are the angels of 8:2, and what is the meaning of the angel and censer in 8:3–5?

26. In the seals the devastation is one quarter, but in the trumpets it is one third. What is the point of this?
27. There are no "woes" in the seals. Why are the last three trumpets identified as "woes"?
28. After the imagery from the plagues against Egypt, why is the river in 9:14 the Euphrates and not the Nile, as one might expect?

Conclusion

In summary, we see that the trumpets are parallel to the seals both in terms of themes and overall pattern. We see John's method of recapitulation at work. In the first four elements of each septet, respectively, we are told the effect of the Fall on humanity, and then the effect of the Fall on nature. In the fifth seal we see that the focus is on humanity's inhumanity and the cry for justice against the wicked. In the sixth seal the subject is the just judgment of God on all humanity, but with the object of pointing to the salvation of the just. In the fifth and sixth trumpets, the focus is on the mercy of God, bringing the theme of humanity's need for redemption into sharper focus. In these two trumpets, the emphasis is on God's forbearance in bringing sinners to repentance. This is why he permits them to be chastised. The seventh of both series has the consummation of the kingdom of God as its focus, with the seventh trumpet filling out the picture beyond what we told in the seventh seal. In addition, in both septets of the seals and trumpets, we clearly see the theme of the cosmic battle: humanity, nature, and angelic and divine beings are all involved in a struggle for humanity's soul.

The themes of a new exodus and a new exile for God's people are struck in the trumpets. Remember, John is a prophet who likes to tell this new portion of salvation history in terms of the Old Testament. Prophets before John—Isaiah and Zechariah especially—told the story of the return from exile in Babylon as a new exodus. The God who liberated his people from Egypt with the exodus is the same one who brought them back from the exile. This is the very same God who made the "land vomit out" his people (Lev 18:24–30), sending them into exile because they made pacts with the inhabitants of the earth (Judg 2). This is also the same God who created the heavens and the earth and is therefore worthy of all worship. His almighty power creates and re-creates. Thus the seals and trumpets follow logically upon Revelation 4 and 5, and conversely, we can see why the themes are what they are: a preparation for these first two septets. As a result of the Fall, humanity is alienated from one another and is clearly disordered in its relationship to the Creator, which shows in worship. Revelation suggests that fallen humanity is prone to idolatry (e.g., Exod 32) and therefore in great need of God's forbearance and mercy. God calls his enemies and the seven churches alike to repentance (Rev 2—3). All of humanity is worthy of God's judgment (sixth seal), but God desires the salvation of all. He directs woeful chastisements against unrepentant idolaters to bring them to repentance and thereby to salvation.

Throughout Revelation John has cleverly cast his contemporary situation in the dress of the ancient stories of salvation. The chief enemies of God's people in the Old Testament are the Egyptians, the Babylonians, and the inhabitants of the earth (the latter often used of the Canaanites). John speaks of the contemporary enemies of God's people, the Romans in particular, in ways and images that immediately bring these ancient foes to mind, so as to encourage his fellow sufferers in Christ. As God liberated and saved his people of old, so too will he do so once again. God's providential care is still active in the face of rampant evil. John is telling the same story, thus the persecuted faithful can take comfort because they already know how the Old Testament ends.

Section Eight:
Revelation 10:1—11:18

Introduction

The twofold interlude of 10:1–11 and 11:1–13 follows after the sixth trumpet/second woe and precedes the seventh trumpet/third woe. Coming on the heels of the first two woes, chapter 10 sounds a note of urgency "because there will be no more delay" (10:5–6), so that the wicked need to repent immediately and the faithful must remain steadfast. Chapter 11 describes the Church's role in bringing sinners to repentance. The seventh trumpet/third woe is the fulfillment of the mystery of God "announced to his servants the prophets" (10:7). This pattern of a twofold interlude between the sixth and seventh elements of the septet is already familiar from the septet of the seals.

The interlude begins with "another mighty angel coming down from heaven" (10:1), a connection to 5:2, where a mighty angel proclaims, "Who is worthy to open the scroll and break its seals?" This connection to 5:2 is intentional because here in chapter 10 is another scroll. Theologically the connection indicates that in this first part of the interlude the focus is on the fulfillment of God's mysterious plan of salvation and the commissioning of John to prophesy it.

John is told by the angel to eat the scroll in his hand. In the Old Testament, at the beginning of his prophetic ministry, Ezekiel eats a scroll given to him by God (Ezek 3:1–3). In this case too, the consumption of a scroll is symbolic of the acceptance of a prophetic mission. The prophet is to speak God's word to his people, and so the scroll is devoured. Since the mouth is the organ of speech, the words of prophecy are symbolically given to the prophet to speak by devouring a scroll. But authentic prophecy is often rejected by God's people, and so although

God's word is sweet as honey to the prophet, it becomes sour in the stomach. John is told to prophesy *again.*

This portion of the interlude, then, reminds the reader that Revelation is a prophecy from God, once *again* announcing God's mysterious plan of salvation. It must be received as such, and blessed are they who accept it (1:3). John's apocalyptic prophecy formally began with the inaugural vision of chapter 1 (similar to Ezekiel's inaugural vision; see Ezek 1—2) and now it continues. Lest we forget it is divine prophecy, we are reminded of that here in this commissioning scene. John is only to reveal what God tells him to, and so the seven thunders—another septet—are sealed up, that is, *not* to be revealed.

Revelation 11:1–13, the second part of the trumpets' interlude, describes the prophetic activity of the Two Witnesses, who are clearly symbolic. Once again, the faithful are seen preserved, by the measuring of the temple and those who worship there. There is no more delay in the advent of the kingdom, so now is the time for witnessing (or giving testimony); note the urgency here. It is urgent because the opportunity for repentance is now, for the end is imminent. The seven thunders are sealed up. They are usually interpreted to be a septet that would have had plagues wreaking havoc on one half of the cosmos, but they remain sealed: the opportunity for repentance initiated by chastisements is past, but the time for repentance as a result of witnessing has arrived. Once the witness to Christ is accomplished, then the seventh trumpet will sound (10:7). With the sounding of the seventh trumpet the mysterious plan of God will be fulfilled. This is no completely new plan but one the Old Testament prophets knew, namely, the salvation of the just and the damnation of the wicked—hence the urgency. John's prophecy will announce this plan once again, and there is no time to lose in doing so (notice the *must* of 10:11; it is necessary because there is no more delay).

The Two Witnesses are portrayed here as enjoying divine protection from the inhabitants of the earth (11:10) and the nations (11:9) while carrying out their necessary duty toward them (11:5). When these Witnesses do God's will, giving testimony (11:4–12), they undergo suffering similar to Christ's (11:7–8) and enjoy a similar glory (11:11–12)—a foreshadowing of the eventual triumph of the faithful. The world's reaction to their "witness of Jesus" will also be the same: the nations will stare and not repent (11:9) and the inhabitants of the earth will rejoice in their death (11:10). The Two Witnesses' testimony, however, is not without effect, for the majority (nine tenths) of the nations do repent (11:13). Thus, the second part of this interlude corresponds to the second part of the seals' interlude. The nations are portrayed as repenting; it is not merely assumed from the vision (as in 7:9). In keeping with the seer's emphasis on repentance and obstinacy in the trumpets' septet, the inhabitants of the earth do *not* repent but even gloat.

In the seventh trumpet (11:15–18), there is a recapitulation of a main theme of the seventh seal, namely, the salvation of the faithful. Although the seventh trumpet is also the third woe (10:7; 11:14–19), it describes the salvation of the faithful as the silence in heaven does in 8:1–2. The seventh trumpet, therefore, appears to be an elaboration of the seventh seal, while at the same time describing *only the beginning* of the kingdom's final consummation. We can expect the completion of its consummation to be told later. The seventh trumpet also elaborates on the seventh seal in addressing the reality of the third woe: the other side of salvation of the just is judgment on the wicked. The judgment and wrath of God brings damnation to the unrepentant sinner.

Questions

29. Is the scroll of chapter 10 the same one that is given to the Lamb in chapter 5, with the seven seals?
30. Who exactly are the Two Witnesses?
31. What is the overall meaning of this interlude?
32. What is the significance of 1,260 days and 42 months?
33. What is the meaning of the temple and its being measured?
34. Why does the seventh trumpet seem a little anticlimactic, especially after 10:7 and 11:14?

Conclusion

This twofold interlude fits nicely between the sixth and seventh trumpets, much the same way as the twofold interlude of seals fits between its sixth and seventh elements. This interlude serves to elaborate on the role God's people plays in the salvation of the world: they must prophesy, announcing the Good News and the need for repentance, and they must bear witness in their lives of faith in order to encourage repentance. The chastisements of the fifth and sixth trumpets with the first and second woes are meant to bring about repentance, *but by themselves they have not.* What is needed now, therefore, at this urgent moment is for the faithful followers of the Lamb to bear witness collectively, in *imitatio Christi* to help bring this about. They do so by the blood of the Lamb, not by their own power. Further chastisements, therefore, like the seven thunders, are not unleashed, because they are no longer needed. The time for salvation and judgment has come, and so there is no more delay, and the seventh trumpet sounds after the prophecy and witness of the Church is at last completed. The Church as the new Israel is to be a light to the nations. The Church, like Elijah and Moses, calls the faithful to adhere stead-fastly to the (new) covenant and to bring idolaters to the worship of the living God. This is part of the sharper focus this septet provides beyond the seals. It is the same two groups in this interlude as in the seals' interlude that make up the elect, the true Israel and the repentant nations. The openness to repentance, typical of the nations, is brought to the fore here. Once again the bottom line in Revelation is hope, not doom. The gist of the seventh trumpet for the persevering faithful is hope in God's holy justice. This trumpet's woefulness pertains only to those hard of heart who refuse to repent.

Thus, the seventh trumpet fills out the picture of the salvation of the faithful. Salvation dawns with the coming of the Anointed One and the consummation of his reign (11:15–16). This advent will ultimately involve a divine visitation and punishment on the wicked, only briefly mentioned in 11:18. God's great day of wrath and judgment will arrive with the final consummation of the kingdom. We can expect that John's vision will not stop with the seventh trumpet since it relates only the beginning of the kingdom's consummation, which is only the beginning of the end, so to speak.

Review of
Revelation 8:2—11:18

As with the previous septet, in the seven trumpets several major themes typical of the book appear. The continuing theme of the effect of the Fall is found, this time with the focus on nature and the angelic world. The theme of repentance/unrepentance predominates. The advent of the consummation of the kingdom of God, with salvation for the faithful, is also a key theme here, put in terms of a new exodus and exile. The emphasis on the plagues of Egypt drives home the new exodus theme, and the Euphrates element likewise drives home the new exile motif. As in the seals, the salvation envisioned here is universal ("many peoples and nations and languages and kings"). One of the book's favorite themes, that God's providence rules the cosmos, is also clearly in evidence here: God limits evil (one third), saves the just, and mercifully encourages the conversion of sinners, especially those who refuse him due worship. The cosmic battle between good and evil is intensified.

The seven trumpets, like the seals, are not all about the end of the world. However, like the seals, their overall orientation is directed to the perfection of all things in Christ, in the final consummation of the kingdom of God, and in the complete defeat of evil. Once again, the trumpets confirm that the book really is all about the ultimate Christian hope, not doom and disaster.

Overall, humanity's dire need of mercy and redemption is highlighted in this septet. If plagues like those carried out against Egypt in the exodus were decisively effective in bringing sinners to repentance, there would be no need for the work of the Lamb or the Church. What the trumpets do beyond the seals is to illustrate the role of the Church in God's mysterious plan of salvation. The prophecy of the Old Testament is not enough. Certainly, however, the Old Testament prophecy, the plagues, and the testimony of the Lamb taken together bring humanity to authentic worship of the living and true God and into the reign of his Anointed One. The new exodus and exile themes in both the seals and the trumpets underscore this subtle point. From of old, God planned to save humanity with its help: therefore not just the Lamb, but also his followers, as the new people of God (the Church) are necessary for the world's salvation. The work of the Church, symbolized by the Two Witnesses, is simply the extension of the Lamb's work in the world. Recall too that Revelation's opening vision is the risen and exalted Christ *present in the Church.*

There is also a replacement motif here, typical of Johannine theology. In the Gospel of John, Jesus replaces the Jewish feasts with himself (he is the Passover Lamb). In chapter 11, we see that the Church as the preserved temple and altar of God is the new Israel; the old people of God (the Jews) has been replaced by this new people, gathered from every tribe, language, people, and nation. Thus, the saints in heaven in the interlude of the seals are from all ethnic groups; here in the trumpets' interlude, the saints on earth—that is, the faithful followers of the Lamb—are also from various ethnic groups, comprising a kingdom rather than a single nation or ethnic group *(ethnos)*. The Church's multicultural diversity foreshadows the heavenly community. Like the former people of God, the new people are a royal kingdom of priests (Rev 1:6; 5:9–10) formed in the new covenant made by the blood of the Lamb. Their hope is to participate fully in the Lamb's reign, when it is finally and fully consummated (11:15–18).

The motif of prophecy and witness by the Church is a new theme, one that fleshes out the work of the Lamb. The little scroll is the participation of the Church as it helps to carry out the redemptive plan of the Lamb in the world, to bring sinners to salvation. As in the seals, what we have here in this septet, then, is also not unfamiliar, but typical biblical themes, dressed in apocalyptic clothing.

In summary, in the septet of the seven trumpets, a pattern becomes evident:

First through fourth trumpets: Natural devastation of one third
Fifth and sixth trumpets: Unnatural demonic devastation of one third (first two woes)

Interlude
Seventh trumpet/third woe: Triumph and judgment

With the seventh trumpet we come to the conclusion of a main section. Below is an outline of Revelation until this point, as well as, for the sake of convenience, material yet to be covered:

I. Prologue (1:1–3): Title, origin, and purpose of Revelation

II. Chapters 1:4—3:22: Introduction and exhortations
   A. Epistolary-prophetic introduction (1:4–20)
   B. Letters to the seven churches (2:1—3:22)

III. Chapters 4:1—22:5: Apocalyptic visions to prepare and strengthen the faithful for the consummation of the kingdom of God
   A An open door in heaven (4:1—11:18)
      1. God enthroned is worthy of worship (4:1—5:14)
      2. Septet of the seals (6:1—8:2)
      3. Septet of the trumpets (8:2—11:18)
   B The temple of God in heaven opens, ark of the covenant is seen (11:19—15:4)
      1. A great sign in heaven, and another sign (11:19—14:20)
      2. Another sign in heaven (15:1–4)
   B′ The temple of the tent of witness in heaven opened (15:5—19:10)
      1. Septet of the bowls (15:5—16:21)
      2. Babylon Appendix (17:1—19:10)
   A′ Heaven opened, the heavenly Rider-Warrior conquers (19:11—22:5)
      1. Victory of God's kingdom (19:11—20:15)
      2. God's covenantal dwelling with the faithful (21:1–8)
      3. Jerusalem Appendix (21:9—22:5)

With Revelation 11:19, a new section begins.

REVELATION
11:19—15:4

Revelation's third septet starts in 15:5, but meanwhile there is other important material. Revelation 11:19—15:4 is an extended introduction to this next septet. This new section is intended to emphasize the protection, patient endurance, and eventual triumph of the faithful followers of the Lamb. It is essentially an elaboration on the Two Witnesses, the Church in its mission of extending the Lamb's work of salvation to the world. This new section also foreshadows the fall of Babylon, the final destruction of unrepentant evildoers, the last battle, and the last judgment. At the end of this section, the next septet is introduced: seven angels holding the bowls are described as another great portent (15:1), a clear reference to the first portent, the Woman clothed with the sun (12:1). These portents (or signs) frame this section.

We now move into another main section of the apocalypse proper of 4:1—22:5, outlined as follows:

> B The temple of God in heaven opens, ark of
>   covenant is seen (11:19—15:4)
>   1. A great sign in heaven, and another sign
>   (11:19—14:20)
>   2. Another sign in heaven (15:1–4)

This main section also introduces the septet of the bowls:

> B' The temple of the tent of witness in heaven opened
>   (15:5—19:10)
>   1. Septet of the bowls (15:5—16:21)
>   2. Babylon Appendix (17:1—19:10)

71

Recall that at various points, John gives indications that either a new vision or section has begun. At four key places—namely, 4:1; 11:19; 15:5; and 19:11—there are verbal markers signaling clear structural divisions that comprise four major sections of the apocalypse proper. These form an ABB′A′ chiasm demarcated by the mention of something in heaven, or heaven itself being opened. It is the second two verbal markers that concern us here: 11:19 and 15:5 form the inner part of this chiasm, the "B" elements. In 11:19 God's temple in heaven is opened and the ark of the covenant is seen there. In 15:5 the temple of the tent of witness in heaven is opened. The ark of the covenant is a primary element in the exodus story; it is there the covenant (the Decalogue) is kept, and there God dwells. The tent of witness is where the ark was housed. John is continuing his new exodus theme. From John's structure and theology it is clear that this new section does not start at 12:1, but rather at 11:19. The relationship of the "B" elements is a literary hinge that connects the septet of the bowls to the material of 11:19—14:20.

Furthermore, in 12:1, 3 and in 15:1 there are three portents (or signs; in Greek, *semeia,* a favorite Johannine word, which the New Revised Standard Version translates as "signs" in the Fourth Gospel) that appear in heaven: the first is the Woman clothed with the sun, the second is a great red Dragon, and the third, the seven last plagues (or bowls). These are the only three signs in Revelation. John uses them in addition to verbal markers to bind 11:19—14:20 together and to indicate a structural division. The first and third signs are described by John as "great," indicating both a literary and theological relationship. The use of the word *signs* recalls the exodus since it was with signs and wonders that God delivered his people of old from Egypt. Thus the new exodus theme is rather prominent here.

We expect the septet of the bowls to now cause complete devastation because the chastisements have destroyed, respectively, one quarter and then one third of the world (11:19—15:4); however, the next step, the anticipated destruction of half the world, is never taken. John first addresses the contemporary situation of the new people of God. The major figures were introduced in the interlude of chapter 11: the Two Witnesses (the Church) and the

Beast. In 11:19—15:4 the earthly war that is part of the great cosmic battle is now described in detail. Put in other terms, the specific urgent reason for a new exodus and exile is now narrated.

The immediate impetus for John's sending his prophetic apocalypse to the churches will now be unveiled. The reason for the book's opening vision of Christ as imperator-king (and not, say, as a shepherd) and for the exhortations of the seven letters will become clear. With 4:1—11:18, the first major portion of the apocalypse proper, John has laid the groundwork of describing the present ordeal of his fellow sufferers in Christ. That the cosmos is corrupt and sinful because of the Fall of humanity; that humanity stands in need of redemption; that the Church has a necessary role in the Lamb's work of saving humanity; that the Church has been commissioned to call itself and the world to repentance by its prophecy and witness; and that the Church will be severely persecuted for this essential work on behalf of the world's redemption—all these things have been established, made clear, and emphasized in chapters 10 and 11. What John will now do is reveal how events will unfold, elaborating more fully on individuals and their interaction in the present corrupt age, and foretelling the ultimate resolution.

Section Nine:
Revelation 11:19—12:18

Introduction

Nowhere else in the book is John's cosmological perspective more clearly portrayed in a dramatic and mythological style than in this section. Revelation is filled with monsters, dragons, and other fantastic creatures both heavenly and demonic. The violent cosmic struggle between good and evil is vividly depicted, while the typical biblical portrayal of peoples as feminine cities is an essential part of the narrative.

John's vision of reality is completely christocentric ("Christ-centered"). For him, the world that rejects Christ, or that promotes compromise in a life otherwise devoted to him, belongs to Satan, the Ancient Serpent, who has been seducing the world since its creation (12:8). Thus, John simply divides all of humanity into two kinds of people: those who live in fidelity to Christ and those who do not. The latter reject him. To put it in terms of Revelation's narrative: one either serves Christ or worships the Beast. There is no gray area, no middle ground; adherence to the truth or seduction into falsehood is all there is in the cosmic battle over humanity's soul. John's worldview comes down to whether the cosmos is grounded in goodness and truth or whether evil and falsehood are the basis of reality, as it so often seems. So it is that John continually exhorts the churches to persevere in fidelity to Christ, and to repent if necessary (2:5, 16, 22; 3:3, 19).

It is in this context that John presents God's final destruction of evil and of those whose lives are spent in compromising with or perpetuating it. It is essential for a sound interpretation of Revelation to understand that its viewpoint is neither vengeful nor vindictive, for even though the narrative is filled with battle scenes and violence, these images are mythological and symbolic depictions of the cosmic struggle. As in other mythological narratives, the imagery is not to be taken literally; rather it is meant to excite the imagination and heart to action, like poetry or music. Revelation is telling the great story of God's ultimate defeat of evil, through Christ. It makes use of popular myths of its own day to do so (the archangel Michael and the Dragon). Perhaps today's best examples of using myth as story to convey universal human truths are *Star Wars* and *The Lord of the Rings.*

Star Wars in its depiction of the cosmic struggle of good versus evil makes use of archetypal mythological symbols (e.g., horns and red-and-black-clad figures, light vs. darkness) in ways that need no explanation in order to grasp. So it is with the Book of Revelation in its use of symbols and imagery. No one needs to be told that *The Lord of the Rings* relates truth about human nature (the lust for power, loyalty), even though its story involves fantastic creatures (hobbits, wizards, and orcs). Its message of good and evil is graspable and its depiction palpable, as it is in Revelation. As with *The Lord of the Rings* and other myths, Revelation is great storytelling. One does not have to stop at every scene to analyze the details in order to understand; in fact, the story is better for not doing so. Revelation's symbolism and imagery are likewise meant to be absorbed and felt in the context of the narrative's movement, and not overanalyzed. Of course there are details that need to be analyzed for us who are centuries and cultures removed, in order to understand John's meaning, but we should be wary of a tendency that aims at deconstructing and explaining every last detail (surely Tolkien would not dream of such an approach to *his* myth).

In 11:19—12:18, John is given a deeper insight into the apocalypse entrusted to him. He is no longer peeking through the door of heaven, as it were (4:1), but has gone further in: he now sees into the heavenly temple and finds the ark of the covenant (11:19). God is enthroned on the ark in the temple, and the entire heavenly court renders him perpetual worship. With this ark is revealed the drama of the "Woman clothed with the sun" and her battle with a great red dragon. The Woman and her child are protected by God from the Dragon, who is not only demonic, but Satan himself (12:9). The Woman's identity is much debated, but the simplest way to understand her is that she represents the new people of God, who gave birth to the Messiah, that is, the Church; she is saved and Satan defeated.

The overall point is to put the conflict between the Church and pagan Rome in context. Putting it in terms of the Woman (the Church) as persecuted by Satan (the Dragon) is ingenious and moving. In the middle of the drama is a "flashback" (12:7–12) that tells of the Dragon's first defeat in heaven. This helps explain his fury in persecuting the Woman on earth. The text of chapters 10 and 11 now makes more sense: the Church (who is also the Two Witnesses) is being persecuted by the enemies of God, all part of the great cosmic battle. The reader should try to feel the emotions compelled by the drama, in its characters, plot, climax, and resolution.

Questions

35. Is this "Woman clothed with the sun" Mary, the Mother of God?
36. Why is there a mythological story here? Myths are not true.
37. What is the purpose of 12:7–12? It seems to interrupt the main story.
38. These are the same numbers found in 11:1–3; what is the point here?

Conclusion

Revelation insists that the Church has a salvific role to play in the world (10:11; 11:1–3, 7). The Church is reminded by John that it must be the sacrament of salvation for the unbelieving and idolatrous world, living so as to bring the inhabitants of the earth face to face with the truth in hopes of conversion (2:8–9; 6:9–10; 12:10–17; 18:24; 19:2). This is particularly clear in chapter 11, in the vision of the Two Witnesses, who represent the Church in its ideal work of bearing the prophetic and faithful witness of Jesus in the face of persecution. It is the role of the new people of God as a priestly people to assist in the Lamb's work of salvation (5:9–10; 12:10–12; 19:1–8), which is why the Two Witnesses are so Christ-like. The Church assists in the Lamb's work by its redemptive suffering (6:9–10), but also by maintaining a particular kind of witness. In chapter 12 the Church, represented by the Woman and her offspring, is again depicted as sharing in Christ's work. The Messiah is born from the old people of God (12:1–6). The Woman's additional offspring, the new people of God, are persecuted but are protected by God (12:7–17). The Woman illustrates that the people of God are saved *as a people*, not as individuals. This is in keeping with the fact that the book is addressed to the people of God as a whole, and not to any individual.

As is seen in chapters 11 and 12 together, the Church is the sacrament of salvation, a great sign, by its *imitatio Christi*. The "witness of Jesus" (1:2, 9; 12:11, 17; and twice in 19:10) is Jesus' own witness, which is borne by the people that serve him faithfully. As discussed earlier, the expression *the witness of Jesus* is a phrase that implies both witness *belonging* to Jesus (object) and the witness *Jesus himself gives* (subject). This dual meaning is important for interpreting John's theology correctly, since Jesus is described in this book as *the* Witness (1:5; 3:14; 22:20).

For John the faithful people of God bear Jesus' own person and work; the Paschal Mystery continues to live and effect salvation in his Body in a mystical way. The Church's witness of Jesus means that those who patiently endure, suffering distress in Jesus, in fact reign with him, They enjoy Jesus' own life *within* them and so *have* and bear that witness that is his, not theirs (1:1–2, 9; 6:9–10; 12:17; 19:10). That is to say, they have Jesus' very own witness, which consists of his giving testimony to the divine love that saves by his life, death, and resurrection. The faithful therefore bear the unique and eternal witness of him who is the "Faithful and True Witness" (1:5), and who alone is worthy to bear that title by virtue of that unrepeatable witness of the cross and resurrection. Those individuals who in turn bear and have the "witness of Jesus" can be called "my faithful witness" by Christ (2:13), because the Paschal Mystery is alive in them, even if (and especially when) they are put to death.

Thus the witness of Jesus is akin to a theological virtue; it is the active empowering of Christ's very presence within the faithful. So while Revelation never speaks in terms of grace, John certainly understands its operation. In its corporate witness of Jesus, the Church is a great sign (portent) of his life, death, and resurrection. This great sign can help people to repentance by extending Christ's saving action in the world. The Two Witnesses of chapter 11 prepare the reader for understanding the Woman in chapter 12 to be the Church, the great sign.

The Church's witness of Jesus and worship of the Lamb are intimately linked. The Mystical Body that bears Jesus' own presence is the new priestly people covenanted in his blood and washed with the blood of Lamb, and undergoing a new exodus so as to serve God as his royal priesthood. Appropriately, this section is introduced in 11:19 with allusions to the covenant at Sinai in the exodus story, where there is meteorological imagery (Exod 19:16), and where the people of God are spoken of as a kingdom of priests (Exod 19:6).

Section Ten:
Revelation 13:1–18

Introduction

The great red Dragon gives up pursuit of the Woman, pursuing instead her offspring. The Dragon then stands on the shore of the sea. This mythological language simply explains that he is continuing to wage war. In biblical literature, the sea is often associated with chaos; it is untamable by human persons, like the primeval chaos of Genesis 1. The first beast (which is the one commonly referred to as "the Beast") comes out of the sea. John is describing the present circumstances of the Church: the Dragon uses the Beast to make war on Christians in the great cosmological battle. Chapter 13 continues the mythological story of chapter 12.

The Beast is clearly a monster, unnatural and demonic, and very much like the Dragon, with seven heads and ten horns. It has the authority of the Dragon (13:2). The Beast together with the Dragon is worshiped by the whole world, meaning particularly all the inhabitants of the earth. The Beast is blasphemous, and rules for the period of three-and-one-half years, the designated time of persecution (compare Dan 7:25; 12:5). It too makes war on the Church throughout the world. Clearly it is in a league with the Dragon.

In addition to the Beast in 13:1–10, there arises a second beast in 13:11–18, who is also demonic and unnatural. This beast comes from the land and has only two horns, but they are ram horns. It too is clearly in league with the Dragon, having its authority and speaking like it. It also works closely with the Beast, working on its behalf and ensuring by signs and deceptions that it is worshiped by the inhabitants of the earth. The typical biblical pairing of land and sea indicates that the Dragon, by means of these two beasts, has the whole world in his grip (13:12).

The two beasts clearly work together. The second one deceives the people into making an idol of the first, then animates the image and causes it to speak. Anyone not worshiping the idol is killed (13:14–15). Also, everyone must be visibly connected to the Beast by bearing its mark on one's head or hand in order to trade or survive in society. This sounds like a story from the tales of Daniel 1 to 6 (especially Dan 2—3), and even more like the apocalyptic section in the second part of Daniel (particularly Dan 8). The apocalyptic section of Daniel tells of persecution of the people of God by a "monster" king using beasts and apocalyptic symbolism. The reader familiar with Daniel's apocalyptic section would not find Revelation 12 and 13 so very different. In fact, it seems that John used Daniel as his model. It is typical of apocalyptic literature to tell of actual persecution in this covert fashion, so as to avoid further attacks. John clearly is describing his contemporary situation in those terms: all must worship the idol set up by the emperor or die. Domitian demanded worship of himself as a god; his statue was to be worshiped, much as the actual historical king in the Book of Daniel (Antiochus IV), and like the pagan kings in Daniel 1 to 6. Domitian had an entire governmental mechanism of priests and officials who promoted and carried out the imperial cult; these are usually identified as the second beast, or false prophet.

John does not explicitly identify the Beast, but rather offers a way for those with a bit of wisdom to figure out who it is. In other words, the Beast represents a person known to John and his contemporaries and who can be identified by the number associated with his name. This infamous number is 666.

John has laid out here the major figures in his drama. What we have in 13:1–18 is a parody of the divine Trinity by a demonic triad: the Dragon, the Beast, and the second beast. Notice that the Beast is described in ways that mimic the Lamb: with a mortal wound that is healed (13:3). It is blasphemous because it tries to usurp Christ's rightful place and claims to be divine though it is not. The Dragon gives the Beast the throne and his authority (13:2), much as the Father gives his throne and kingdom to the

Son. The second beast is to be identified as the false prophet who animates the idol of the Beast and promotes its cult. It is the Spirit, of course, who animates and speaks through authentic prophets among the people of God. By telling the story of the cosmic battle between good and evil in this way, John has offered a profound insight: evil cannot create, it can only mimic. Evil attracts people because it deceives them into thinking it is good (as with the temptation in Gen 3). John has now introduced all of the major players but one. The story, therefore, will continue in chapter 14.

Questions

39. What is the meaning of the infamous 666?
40. Why are the beasts described in this way they and what or whom do they symbolize?
41. Revelation 13:8–10 sounds like predestination. Is it?

Conclusion

The first beast (again, simply the Beast) is the key figure in the forefront of the drama, but the Dragon is the actual power, with the second beast in between the two. This makes sense in terms of a parody, since it is the Beast and the Lamb who are directly engaged in combat. They are the two kings who vie for power; Domitian has self-proclaimed authority over the world, a false power given by the Dragon, who is the prince of this world. The Lamb has all authority over the entire cosmos, given to him by the Father. He is also King of All Kings, with true and almighty power. It is the archangel Michael and the Woman who battle the Dragon, though in the end it is God who destroys him. The Beast comes from the abyss (bottomless pit) in 11:7 and 17:8, which appears to be its residence after having arisen from the sea. This abyss is where Satan (the Dragon) and the fallen angels dwell after having been defeated by Michael and driven out of heaven.

John is describing here in chapters 12 and 13 the Church's part in the great cosmic battle. In the seven letters to the churches, there was always the promise of reward for those who are victorious (who "conquer"). Here John depicts why: in war, the spoils go to the victors. Evil must be defeated in order for the kingdom of God to be finally and perfectly consummated. The "Christ event" began that process, and now it is continued with the Two Witnesses, the Church.

Section Eleven:
Revelation 14:1—15:4

Introduction

In 14:1 there is a clear division marker for a new section ("then I looked and there was..."). This section extends until 15:5, where the next septet and major portion of the book will begin. Chapters 14:1—15:4 are the last segment of the major portion that began with 11:19. Thus, it continues John's portrayal of the present situation of the Church. We have been introduced, on the one hand, to the Woman clothed with the sun and her offspring (including the Messiah), and to the demonic triad that parodies the divine Trinity, on the other. These two sides are engaged in a cosmic struggle over humanity's soul. We also know that the situation is urgent, since the Dragon is furiously raging upon the earth, and the faithful face martyrdom for refusing to worship his primary instrument of deception and enslavement, the Beast.

John has, however, already foreshadowed how the story ends. The Woman is protected by God for the period of persecution (three-and-one-half years); thus we know that the Church will ultimately be victorious over Satan. We also know that individual Christians are not only called to conquer him, but they will be victorious over Satan by the blood of the Lamb and by the word of their testimony, not clinging to life even in the face of death (12:11). The victory of the persevering faithful will often consist in martyrdom rather than avoiding it. Martyrdom is not defeat for the people of God, but a mighty weapon in the arsenal to conquer the Dragon.

In 14:1–5, John sees the Lamb on Mount Zion with a vast army of the faithful. Together with the Lamb, this army will defeat the Beast. Yet no battle is described, only the amassing of troops in preparation for the battle. Once again, we have to wait until later for the story to be told in full. For now, John portrays a confrontation: the Dragon, taking his stand by the sea, and the Lamb with his army, standing on Mount Zion. Evil and chaos are opposed to goodness and salvation.

In 14:6–13, which is a new vision, John sees and hears three angels make proclamations. The first announces the Gospel calling humanity to repentance, for the time of judgment has arrived. The second announces the fall of Babylon as a result of divine judgment. The third announces the wrath of God on those idolaters who worship the Beast. These proclamations are followed by prophetic sayings in 14:12–13.

In 14:14–20, there is a twofold harvest scene. In the first part, 14:14–16, the Son of Man reaps the harvest of the whole earth, an image of judgment. In the second, 14:17–20, an angel harvests the grapes of wrath of the earth, also an image of judgment. Behind this twofold harvest image are Old Testament passages of vintage and harvests, symbolizing divine wrath and judgment on unrepentant sinners (especially Joel 4 and Isa 63).

In Revelation 15:1–4, the final septet of the bowls (or plagues) is introduced. These verses clearly go with the preceding section rather than the following one because of certain verbal hinges. Much as 8:2 is a literary hinge connecting the seals and the trumpets, so too is 15:1 a literary hinge. There is a major verbal connection between the great sign (portent) in heaven of 12:1, the Woman clothed with the sun, and the seven angels with the seven plagues of 15:1. The great sign in heaven of 15:1 is also "amazing" or "wondrous," language reminiscent of the signs and wonders of the plagues against Egypt in exodus (e.g., Ps 135). Revelation 15:1 introduces the seven last plagues, which will begin at 15:5. In 8:2 the trumpets are introduced, but they are sounded only beginning in 8:6 after a short explanatory scene. Now in 15:2–4 there is a similar short explanatory scene before the unleashing of the bowls in 15:5, though in 15:1 they are introduced. Such a pattern, of course, tells the reader there is a connection between what precedes and follows. That is to say that the bowls are connected to the material in chapters 12 to 14. In fact, 15:5 will make that plainer.

In 15:1–4, the faithful who are victorious over the Beast are seen singing God's praises in a song of "Moses and...of the Lamb." Juxtaposed to the two previous scenes of judgment there is now a scene of salvation. As mentioned earlier, Revelation never presents only humanity's doom; with judgment there is mercy and salvation. Chapters 14:1—15:4 are a complete unit: the opening scene of the Lamb and his army, together with the victorious faithful, frame the inner scenes of the three angels and the harvests of judgment. This framing suggests that the theology of John is one of consolation and hope to those who resist the Beast and remain steadfast in the word of God and the witness of Jesus, because the Lamb will defeat the Beast. The inner scenes are not meant to terrify, but rather to exhort the sinner, the idolater, and all who give allegiance to the Beast to repent lest they are trampled in the grapes of divine wrath and suffer eternal damnation.

Questions

42. What is the meaning of the Lamb on Mount Zion with an army of 144,000 virgins?
43. What is the role of the three angels and their pronouncements? Are they connected to the three woes of the trumpets?
44. Why are there two parts to the harvest scene?
45. What is the meaning of the scene and song in 15:2–4?

Conclusion

Revelation 14:1—15:4 can be outlined as follows:

14:1–5	Lamb's army on Mount Zion
14:6–13	Three angels and prophetic sayings
14:14–20	Twofold harvest scene
15:1	Seven angels with seven last plagues
15:2–4	Conquerors of the Beast on a fiery sea of glass

The Messianic Lamb, who is the Passover Lamb, provides a new exodus for those who follow him faithfully wherever he goes. After battling the tyrant, he brings them through the Red Sea to his kingdom, the new promised land. The fiery sea may signify that passage into this kingdom at the hand of the Beast is to pass into by martyrdom; certainly it is by the blood of the Lamb. An overall theme here is the perfect consummation of God's kingdom, for which the complete destruction of evil must take place first. This is done by the Lamb and his army, who wage war against the Dragon and the Beast. The new exodus theme reminds the persecuted Church that God will bring his people to himself where they will be a kingdom of priests, covenanted with him in the blood of the Lamb, who is also their commander-king.

Here again John calls the faithful to continued patient endurance, one of Revelation's favorite virtues. They must witness to the truth in Christ and not compromise by worshiping the Beast. The battle over humanity's soul is put in terms of truth and falsehood, as it is in the Fourth Gospel. The Church must witness to the truth of Christ, helping to carry on his redemptive work, for the salvation of the nations. The worshipers of the Beast are embroiled in lies and deception. The present matter of whom to worship is urgent, for the judgment is imminent and the harvest is ready to reap.

Review of Revelation 11:19—15:4

Revelation 4:1—11:18 tells of humanity's corruption and Fall, its just judgment and salvation (seals), the corruption of the rest of the natural world (first four trumpets), and such supernatural creatures as angels (fifth and sixth trumpets). The seventh trumpet, like the seventh seal, speaks briefly of the consummation of God's kingdom, highlighting salvation with a new and final exodus theme. The interludes of both the seals and the trumpets introduce the reader to the elect, who are protected and saved by God in reward for their fidelity. The little scroll and the Two Witnesses emphasize the role of the Church in continuing the redemptive work of the Lamb in the world. Repentance of the nations and idolaters is also emphasized.

The recapitulation technique is at work in these two septets, with progression in the details: the trumpets, especially the woes, are more devastating than the seals. The role of the followers of the Lamb (the Church) in the salvation of the world is told in a condensed fashion so as to highlight the need for prophecy, witness, and fidelity to Christ in the cosmic battle. All this prepares for 11:19—15:4, which essentially describes the Church's current situation.

The Church is caught up in the cosmic battle, which is told in a mythological way. The enemies of God and his people—that is, the opponents of the Lamb and his followers—insist on idolatry or death. They reject the truth of God for the falsehood of Satan. The Dragon wages war and conquers individual Christians, though the Church herself (symbolized in the Woman) endures. The Church conquers its enemies by the blood of the Lamb. The Dragon and the Lamb face off, with battle lines drawn. The Dragon stands by the sea, with chaos; the Lamb's army stands on Mount Zion, with goodness. The matter is urgent, for the final battle is about to begin. The whole cosmos is involved, with all of humanity called to heed the eternal Gospel. The harvest is ready: the Son of Man will gather the faithful into his messianic kingdom, and the cup of the wrath of God will be drunk by unrepentant sinners.

The overarching theme here is the new exodus made possible by the blood of the Lamb. At long last, God is bringing his faithful people into the new promised land, the kingdom of his Anointed One. The Church is brought by God to the desert where she is provided for and protected by him while the Passover Lamb and his army wage a messianic war against the Dragon. When they are victorious, a new song of Moses and the Lamb is sung to praise the holiness, justice, and goodness of God.

Revelation 11:19 commences a new major section of the apocalypse proper, which will conclude in 19:10. In 11:19—15:4 there is an important portrayal of the major issue John and his fellow suffers face: the enraged Dragon is waging war against the Woman and her offspring, which encompasses the Lamb's army. Revelation 4:1—11:18 was preparatory to this key event. We can expect that the rest of this major section will be about the outcome of this war between the Woman and her offspring and the Dragon.

The next major section and septet starts in 15:5, and the great sign of 15:1 is a clear reference to the first one, the Woman clothed with the sun (12:1). Revelation 11:19—15:4 is the introduction to the bowls, intended to emphasize the protection, patient endurance, and eventual triumph of the elect while they are suffering persecution and are embroiled in spiritual warfare. This section also foreshadows the fall of Babylon, the final destruction of evildoers, the last battle, and the final judgment. Revelation 11:19—15:4 is a bridge connecting the seven trumpets and the seven bowls, providing an extensive elaboration on the meaning of both.

REVELATION
15:5—19:10

In 15:5—16:21, John presents the final septet, the bowls of God's wrath. In 15:1 John describes them as final plagues and as "another great portent in heaven," like that of the Woman in 12:1. This other heavenly sign brings God's wrath to fulfillment by justly punishing the enemies of the Woman and her offspring.

These bowls are the plagues that bring God's wrath to fullness, and so they complete the judgment and justice of God. As such they inflict 100 percent devastation rather than one quarter or one third as in the previous septets. Those septets were meant as chastisements, a divine pedagogy meant to encourage and teach repentance. The bowls are different. They are judgments punishing the willfully unrepentant. These bowl-plagues will usher in the consummation of the kingdom of God when the reign of the Beast is destroyed. They are like the tenth plague against Egypt, that is, they liberate God's people and crush their stubborn oppressors. Those who worship the Beast will be punished by being made to drink the blood of the cup of God's wrath, which is fitting and just, given they shed the blood of those who refused to worship the Beast but instead worshiped the only true God (16:6–7). God's holiness and justice demand no less; his enemies get what they are literally worthy of (NRSV 16:6 reads "what they deserve").

In 17:1—19:10, John presents an expansive description of the fall of Babylon, which is explicitly connected to the seven bowls by 17:1. Babylon-Rome, portrayed as the great Harlot, is the city of evildoers and those who worship the Beast, especially the inhabitants of the earth (17:2, 8). The fall of Babylon is presented as just punishment (18:21–24). Revelation 19:1–10 is a transitional scene meant to emphasize God's just judgment of the Harlot and to celebrate (liturgically) the corresponding salvation of the just, whom the Harlot has persecuted and killed. The victory of God over the Harlot means the ascension to the throne by the Lamb, with his coronation also being his wedding day. Those who serve God faithfully are invited to the great nuptial feast.

Section Twelve:
Revelation 15:5—16:21

Introduction

Although the bowls actually begin in 15:5, they are introduced in 15:1 as seven last plagues, "for with them the wrath of God is ended." The pattern of the septet of the bowls is similar to that of the seals and the trumpets, but there are dissimilarities designed to get the reader's attention and to make theological points. For example, this septet does not have a separation of its first four elements from the last three. Moreover, it is preceded by a vision of the triumph of the faithful (15:1–4), which is particularly arresting since the reader has just been told that these plagues bring God's wrath to an end. However, this is precisely the point John wishes to convey, namely, that the consummation of the kingdom entails the complete destruction of evil.

Throughout the seven bowls, the reader is repeatedly reminded of this. There is no interlude in this septet. This factor, along with the rapid succession of each of the seven bowls—one following immediately upon the other, without the first four being noticeably set off from the last three—sounds a note of rapid intensity and definitude. It also indicates the set purpose and mighty execution of God's holy will. There is no mistaking that his wrath is given vent or that this is indeed the end of evil. There is also no more time for preparation or witness by the Church; there is no vision or mention of the sealing of the faithful.

The portrayal of the Church as already victorious over the Beast (15:2) and of the nations as repentant (15:3), in the context of the judgment of God revealed (15:4), serves to highlight that those who willfully refuse to fear God and glorify the Lord's name are finally destroyed. There is no more delay of divine justice, and the distress depicted in this septet is only of evildoers. In this septet, the contrast between the reward already won by the faithful in the introduction (15:1–4) and the punishment of the ungodly emphasizes the glory and power of God (15:5–8; 16:9), together with his holy justice.

Thus, with the bowls, the focus is no longer on God's mercy and patience but on his holiness, justice, and might (16:5–7). God calls forth the angels to release severe plagues on the earth, which are said to be explicitly directed against those who worship the Beast (16:2, first bowl). The second and third bowls particularly echo the plagues against Egypt in the exodus and proclaim the justice and holiness of God in punishing the enemies of God and his people. In the fourth bowl, those whose hearts are hardened blaspheme the Almighty rather than repent (16:9). The fifth bowl is a direct blow to the throne of the Beast, and those who worship him blaspheme God but do not repent (16:10–11). The worshipers of the Beast are none other than the inhabitants of the earth, who still not only refuse to repent but grow even more obstinate, cursing God. Their suffering gives rise to contempt of God rather than repentance, and so they blaspheme him (16:21). Like Pharaoh in Egypt in the exodus account, these willfully unrepentant sinners are punished by wrathful plagues.

The sixth bowl is the great final (eschatological) battle (16:14), which is described again more fully in 19:11—20:15. With the seventh bowl the plagues are finished (16:17). As in the seventh seal and seventh trumpet, the seventh bowl depicts the end of evil's reign in the world and the complete consummation of the kingdom. But the description is more vivid in this final septet, even if brief: there is the greatest earthquake ever, by which the cities of the nations and Babylon are destroyed, and the events associated with the great day of the Lord are mentioned (16:18–20). Strangely, however, there is no mention of God's dwelling with his people in his kingdom as in the previous septets. The elaborate description of the everlasting presence of God with the faithful is delayed until all the horrid details of the defeat of Satan and his followers are completely given.

Questions

46. In 15:5–8 there is a tent of witness in a heavenly temple that becomes filled with smoke from the glory of God, so that no one can enter until the plagues are over. What does this mean?

47. Why are the angels in 15:6 dressed in pure white linen with gold sashes across their chests?

48. Why are theses plagues identified as the plagues of the seven angels and not the bowls? Why are the bowls golden and poured out?

49. What are the similarities of the bowls to the plagues of Egypt in the exodus?

50. The sixth and seventh bowls seem to have a Babylonian motif. Explain.

51. What exactly is Armageddon (16:16)?

52. Are the sixth and seventh bowls the end of the world?

53. What is the significance of the great city Babylon? Since it did not exist as a great city in the first century is it "only" a symbol?

Conclusion

The major themes in this section jump off the page: the just and holy judgment of God, the new exodus and exile, and willful unrepentance. The hymn in this section is interpretive, a literary technique John often uses in Revelation. The angel of the third bowl praises God for being just and holy. It is in this very justice and holiness that God's judgment is rendered; judgment is no mere arbitrary thing. The holiness of God demands that unrepentant sinners and idolaters be judged. They are also judged for persecuting and killing God's people (16:6). They get a just punishment: they must drink the blood God gives them to drink because they shed innocent blood. This is not vindictiveness but justice (the fifth seal), for they reap what they sowed. The blood they wrongly shed is, however, not the blood of the grape. The latter is merely what is used as the image for judgment.

The cup of God's wrath (14:19) is a common image for his judgment; it makes people reel and stagger (e.g., Ps 75:9; Jer 25:15). John seems to have Jeremiah's prophecy of the Babylonian exile particularly in view with this image. In Jeremiah 25 the prophet is told to take the cup of divine wrath to the nations to drink, and they "shall drink and stagger and go out of their minds, because of the sword that I am sending among them" (Jer 25:16). God tells them to "drink...fall...and to rise no more" (25:27). This cup is specifically directed at Babylon. The blazing wine of his wrath in 16:19 echoes Jeremiah's prophecy.

As in Jeremiah 25, the divine wrath is poured out on the nations here because of their injustice to God's people. The exile is nearly over; Babylon will fall and the exiles will go home. These plagues are modeled on the plagues against Egypt; the tyrant is defeated so God's people can escape to the desert and make their way home to him, their true and benevolent king.

Revelation's plagues are poured out on very specific targets: those marked with the sign of the Beast or who worship its image (first bowl); those who martyred God's people (second and third bowls); humanity in general, specifically blasphemers (fourth bowl); the throne of the Beast and its kingdom (fifth bowl); Babylon itself (sixth bowl). The seventh causes destruction to Babylon and other cities, as well as inflicts punishment on blasphemers. These plagues are all judgments against idolaters and obstinate sinners, like those of the exodus. They are not even chastisements, because the time of delay is over. The saying of the angel in 16:5–7 and the song of Moses and the Lamb in 15:3–4 help the reader understand that now is the time for judgment. Their general context help convey that as well. The bowls of wrath follow on the judgment imagery of the vintage (14:17–20). They also precede the description of the judgment against Babylon as it is carried out (17:1—18:24).

Section Thirteen:
Revelation 17:1—19:10

Introduction

Revelation 17:1—19:10 is often referred to as the Babylon Appendix. It belongs to the septet of the bowls by way of the literary hinge in 17:1, in which one of the angels of the seven bowls invites John to see the great Harlot of Babylon. Chapters 17 and 18 are an extended description of the divine judgment upon her and her consequent demise. Revelation 19:1–10 is commentary on it from a heavenly perspective.

We have already met one people in this text symbolized in feminine terms: the Woman clothed with the sun symbolizes the new people of God, the Church. In the Old Testament, biblical cities are often symbolized in feminine terms, for example., daughter Zion, Mother Jerusalem. John used the hated city of the exile, Babylon, to symbolize Rome, something easily understood by John's contemporaries (see 1 Pet 5:13 and Old Testament prophetic texts like Ezek 16, Isa 47, and Jer 51). John intends to draw a contrast between these two women-cities: the Church is a spotless, pure bride, and Rome, her enemy, is a filthy, corrupt harlot. We will see that the Woman (chap. 12) is also the Bride of the Lamb, which is the city of the new Jerusalem (chap. 21). There is thus a tale of two women here: Rome, which is symbolized by Babylon, and the Church, which is symbolized by the new Jerusalem. This symbolism is intended to evoke emotion and move hearts. In the corrupt world, Christians are being enticed by the great Harlot, but their real allegiance has to be to the Lamb's pure Bride, who is good and loved by God. Evil is seductive and attractive perhaps, but it is rotten on the inside and deadly like a harlot.

In chapter 17, the reason for the divine judgment, already announced in 14:8, is given: Babylon is "drunk with the blood of the saints and the blood of the witnesses to Jesus" (17:6). It is repeated in 18:3: "for all the nations have drunk of the wine of the wrath of her fornication"; and in 18:5: "for her sins are heaped high as heaven." In Domitian's day, the city of Rome was deified as the goddess Roma. Here John is poking fun of such a ridiculous notion by portraying her as a whore. This ridiculing of idols and idolatry is typical of the Old Testament prophets.

The divine judgment of Babylon and its consequences are told in a dirge, or funeral lament, in 18:2–19. The divine command to execute judgment is given in 18:6–7. Those who profited from Babylon-Rome and its corruption (kings, merchants, shippers) will mourn her, but from afar, lest they fall with her. The actual judgment is rendered in 18:20–24. A mighty angel performs a symbolic act of throwing a great millstone into the sea, where it will sit on the bottom unmoved. This stone is Babylon-Rome. The language of her devastation (18:22–23) is that of exile, echoing Jeremiah, chapters 25 and 51, in which the devastation of Jerusalem is told. Babylon-Rome is requited (18:6) for the exile it has inflicted on the new people of God. Thus pagan Rome with its imperial cult and intolerance of Christianity is portrayed as the new Babylon.

In 19:1–10 there is a victory celebration in heaven over the just judgment on God's enemies, in which God is praised for his holy justice. The vanquishing of Babylon ushers in the establishment of God's reign (19:6) and the wedding feast of the Lamb (19:7–9). These joyful hymns stand in contrast to the mournful dirge over Babylon.

In the pagan world of the Roman Empire in John's day, idolatry was the norm as well as the official religion of the state. Jews were permitted by law to keep to their religious traditions and observances, but Christians were not yet allowed legal exemption from idolatry and would not be for several centuries. There were temples to the gods practically everywhere, regular celebrations in honor of the emperor as a god, food in the marketplaces that had been sacrificed to idols, and the like. The pagan cults invariably involved gluttony, drunkenness, and idolatry, all deadly sins to the Church's mind. Most often the worship of idols included ritual prostitution and orgies.

The ritual sacrifices to the gods would involve burning incense and pouring out libations to them (in bowls, an apt image for plagues aimed at idolaters). The drink offering was frequently the fresh blood of slaughtered bulls (e.g., the cult of Mithras). Sometimes it was difficult for pagans who converted to Christianity to give up these practices, especially if they were members of a trade or business guild. These guilds were dedicated to the honor of gods, and business meetings would include feasts in their honor and cultic practices, like ritual prostitution, forbidden by Christian morality. Business loans were made by the temples and guilds (the ancient equivalent of modern banks), and so if one stopped attending the cult or temple of the guild, one might soon be out of business or shunned by the business community. (1 Cor and Acts are full of stories that shed light on these realities.) Being a Christian often meant poverty, and almost certain social marginalization, and so Christians usually had to support one another financially. That the last plagues are libations poured out in judgment on the idolaters of the Beast is fitting. That Babylon-Rome is made to drink the wine of God's wrath is similarly fitting. Rome martyred so many Christians that the blood of the grape becomes symbolic of the wrath of God over the innocent shed blood of his saints.

Notice that God's people are called to come out of Babylon before judgment is executed against her (Rev 18:4; see Jer 50:8). This last admonition is for the "fence-sitters" who have been tempted by her. All those who sin with her will share in her plagues, even Christians.

Questions

54. Why is Babylon-Rome depicted as a harlot?
55. Who are the kings and the scarlet Beast of chapter 17? The angel's explanation to John is convoluted.
56. It makes some sense that the kings would mourn Babylon, but why do merchants and shippers?

57. Why does it take only one hour to destroy Babylon-Rome?
58. What is the meaning of the beautiful image of the wedding feast of the Lamb (19:7–9)?
59. Why, in a book so opposed to idolatry, does John worship an angel (19:10)?

Conclusion

This section is replete with themes. The major ones are the divine wrath justly poured out upon Babylon-Rome; Babylon-Rome's judgment is complete, definitive, and swift; evil is limited and (self-)destructive; the rightful sovereignty of God is finally being accomplished in full; and divine providence is praised.

This vision of the great Harlot is clearly meant by John to be in opposition to the Lamb's Bride, the Woman clothed with the sun, who had fled into the desert where she was protected by God (12:6). The Harlot is also in the desert, where John is brought to see her (17:3). These two symbolic, feminine cities-peoples are facing off in battle in the desert. The desert imagery is a new exodus motif, of course; the mythic imagery and the notion of a cosmic combat are still operative in this section.

Though the great Harlot is judged and destroyed, there is no vindictiveness here (in spite of texts like 18:20, 24; 19:2–3). The judgment is just, and executed by God, who is praised for his just and holy judgments (19:2). The other side of judgment on Babylon-Rome, however, is the salvation of the Woman and her offspring; hence the cry for them to rejoice (18:20). Innocent blood is avenged (19:1–2) and evil is put to routs.

Heaven celebrates the victory of God in defeating his enemies. This section (19:1–10) is similar to that of the celebration in heaven when Michael defeats the Dragon (12:10–12). Now the Beast is being defeated too. With the final vanquishing of evil, God's reign will be fully established—a reason to celebrate, for now the Lord will assume his rightful reign, something for which the entire cosmos groans in longing. God's sovereignty is being exercised in his just and holy will to snuff out evil completely.

Babylon-Rome is judged with a just punishment, that is, with one that fits her crimes. As she has seduced, corrupted, and made others drunk, now she is made to drink and suffer the effects of it. She who had sat enthroned, haughty and blasphemous, now is dethroned and brought low. John tells of her dethronement in terms typical of Old Testament judgment oracles in the prophets, especially of Babylon and Tyre (e.g., Jer 50—51 and Ezek 26—27). God's providence is at work here, caring for the salvation of his people surely, but especially in making good come out of evil: in Revelation 17:17 it is God who moves the wicked to carry out his plan. John is convinced that God is in control of history and the entire cosmos. The vision of the destruction of the great Harlot gives hope to the oppressed and marginalized Christians of John's day and is meant to encourage Christians of every age in the battle against evil. Evil may rule for a time, but it will finally end by God's mighty hand. That same divine hand that brings judgment and justice also dispenses mercy and salvation to those who patiently endure and bear the testimony of Jesus; they are invited to the wedding feast.

Review of
Revelation 15:5—19:10

Before reviewing 15:5—19:10 specifically, it is useful at this juncture to review generally the overall thrust of the three septets of the seals, trumpets, and bowls. The seals appear to open up and overlap with the trumpets (8:1–5), but the trumpets and the bowls do not appear to overlap. There is a clear pattern of similarity in the seals and the trumpets (4 + 2 + interlude + 1), a pattern not shared by the bowls (all seven are in succession without a grouping or an interlude). The bowls have an appendix (17:1—19:10, or two really, as we shall see in 21:1). The seals and trumpets are aimed at moving sinners to repentance, whereas the bowls are just punishments executed against them for their wickedness.

All three septets come from the throne of God and the Lamb. The seals are opened by the Lamb, the trumpets are blown by the seven angels of the presence (8:2), and the bowls are poured out by them (15:1, 5; 16:1). This highlights the fact that God is in control of the cosmos and history, his providence ruling and providing for all things, encompassing both good and evil. All three septets have new exodus and exile motifs.

In the septets of the bowls and trumpets, what is harmed is similar: first the land, then the sea, then the rivers and springs, and afterward the sun. The fifth, sixth, and seventh in both these series are likewise similar: the throne of the Beast is plunged into extreme agony (with darkness and boils), and the demonic locusts that come from the abyss cause extreme agony. In addition, there are three demonic froglike spirits at the Euphrates, and the demonic cavalry is at the Euphrates with three plagues; the end of the realm of evil is spoken of, and the time for "destroying those who destroy" is likewise mentioned.

What do these parallels and similarities mean? Why is the pattern that started with the first two septets not continued in the third, even though the third is so similar to the second (yet without the interlude or formal separation of a 4 + 3 setup)? Each septet has its own meaning, to be sure, but what is the overall thrust of them taken together?

Since Revelation uses a recapitulation technique, there must be an overall theology expressed by it. First, there is told by the three septets the history of creation: from the Fall of humanity, which affects the natural world, to the Fall of angels, which then affects heaven and humanity. The redemption of humanity and creation wrought by God and the Lamb includes both mercy (forbearance in bringing humanity to repent) and just judgment (on the unrepentant).

Second, John places his own contemporary situation in this context of redemption and Fall. Humanity is locked in the great cosmic battle between good and evil. The Church in particular suffers the onslaught of Satan and his partners. She will be victorious if she remains faithful in the witness of Jesus in the blood of the Lamb.

Third, the recapitulating progress of the septets culminates, with the last plague, in the climax of God's wrath against his enemies and those of the Church. John elaborates on the septet of the bowls with an expansive description of the defeat of the Beast and the great Harlot, much as he had elaborated on the seals and the trumpets in chapters 12 to 14. Thus, all three septets are aimed ultimately at describing the final defeat of evil and the consummation of the kingdom of God. With each septet, Revelation's narrative has moved forward, bringing us closer and closer to the perfect consummation of the kingdom. All three septets underscore the heavenly reward that awaits the victorious (7; 8:1; 11:15–8; 12:10–12; 14:1–5; 15:1–4; 19:1–10). These scenes of salvation and heavenly bliss, interspersed at key interpretative intervals, emphasize the real overall message of Revelation: salvation is from the Lamb, given to those who persevere in worshiping him alone.

John's new-exodus and new-exile motifs encourages his fellow Christians to hope in the heavenly promised land, and so to persevere in the faith. The Christian's real citizenship is not in Babylon-Rome or even the earthly Jerusalem; as befitting the offspring of the celestial Bride, it is in the kingdom of her Spouse. John's use of mythology and Old Testament harvest-imagery likewise moves the persecuted Church to remain steadfast in the face of evil as they face possible martyrdom. Taken all together, these septets clearly have hope and salvation as their major outlook, rather than doom and destruction. They are meant to inspire not fear but rather trust in Divine Providence. God's holy and true justice is an instrument of Providence, but so are his patience and mercy.

By the use of these septets and their expansions (11:19—15:4; 17:1—19:10), John has told the story of the cosmos and the Church. The details of the imagery and symbolism are certainly culturally driven, and therefore in need of interpretation by later generations and other cultures (like twenty-first-century Americans), but the basics are readily grasped and assimilated by all, no matter what culture or age, for the cosmic battle continues and the opponents are still the same.

With this last septet there is a definite climax, though its resolution has yet to come. The story of the final vanquishing of the realm of evil and the perfect consummation of the kingdom of God is still to be told, which we expect to see next.

REVELATION
19:11—22:5

In this final section of the apocalypse proper, begun at 4:1, we move from the cycle of septets into the climax of the visions. The apocalyptic-prophetic visions of 4:1—22:5 are intended to prepare and strengthen the faithful as they await the perfect consummation of the kingdom of God.

In this last section, the visions are decidedly eschatological, that is, specifically about the end-days, including human history and the long tyranny of evil. These end-days, of course, also include matters about heaven, hell, death, and judgment. The full consummation of the kingdom involves the definitive and irreversible destruction of evil, which is done by the King of Kings and Lord of Lords, at his Second Coming. God finally places all things under his feet.

This section can be outlined as follows:

1. Long-awaited victory of God (19:11—20:15)
2. God's covenantal dwelling with his people (21:1–8)
3. Jerusalem Appendix (21:9—22:5)

At the beginning of this section, heaven is opened, and the heavenly Rider-Warrior comes forth to conquer Satan, the Beast, and the false prophet (or second beast). With this Second Advent (also known as the *Parousia*), the end-days are brought to completion. In 19:11, there is a direct verbal parallel to 4:1 with the opening of heaven. John is marking out the structural points of his work. Clearly 19:1–10 ends the previous section, and 19:11 begins a new major section.

Revelation 19:11—20:15 provides an elaborate description of the definitive destruction of evil and the perfect consummation of the kingdom. In essence it is a vivid description of the final eschatological battle and the passing away of all things temporal. It is the Word of God as the heavenly Rider-Warrior who conquers the Beast, the false prophet, and their followers (19:11–12). Satan is finally vanquished by God (20:1–10), and the universal last judgment takes place (20:11–15). Once evil has been irreversibly destroyed, the new heaven and new earth are created (21:1–8). It is here that God dwells in his heavenly kingdom with his people (21:3–4). It is only with this vision that God declares the consummation of his kingdom, the entire goal of the Book of Revelation, to be accomplished (21:5–8).

As the Babylon Appendix (17:1—19:10) elaborates on the final judgment against evil depicted in the previous visions of the seven bowls, the Jerusalem Appendix in 21:9—22:5 elaborates on Christ's final victory over evil that is depicted in 19:11—21:8. The contrast between evil and good is made clear by the parallel between 17:1 and 21:9 and the two appendices. Thus the judgment of evildoers is described in the seven bowls, with a corresponding narrative in the Babylon Appendix; the justice-salvation rendered to the faithful is described in 19:11—21:8, with a corresponding narrative in the Jerusalem Appendix.

In the consummating vision of the book (21:9—22:5), the life of the kingdom is depicted as blissful and a continual worship of the Creator, with the nations included (21:24–25; 22:2) and the inhabitants of the earth excluded (21:8, 27). The former repent, but the latter do not. This portion is labeled as the Jerusalem Appendix because the kingdom is described in terms of a new, heavenly Jerusalem. This contrasts, of course, with the wicked earthly city of Babylon-Rome. In the heavenly city of God, the faithful who persevered through persecution and martyrdom will reign with the Lamb and enjoy perfect bliss: no tears, no suffering, no sickness, no death, no evildoers to endure. It is an eternal sabbath rest in the eternal promised land from which God's people will never be exiled.

Revelation 22:1–5 presents the book's central image again, namely, God and the Lamb enthroned, providing a nice inclusion with chapters 4 and 5, which opened this major portion of the book. The faithful are pictured as reigning victoriously forever, as promised in the letters to the cities and foreshadowed in texts like chapter 7. It is the perpetual wedding feast of the Lamb in the new everlasting promised land; the new exodus and exile are over—the Lamb has brought his Bride into his home at last.

Section Fourteen: Revelation 19:11—20:15

Introduction

Revelation 19:1–10 not only concludes the previous section (15:5—19:10), but it also serves as a transition to this new section. After the destruction of Babylon-Rome in chapters 17 and 18, in 19:1–10 God is praised in heaven for his just judgment and defeat of her. He is hailed as king and the wedding day of the Lamb is announced, together with a beatitude on all who are invited to it. What we now expect to see, then, is the reign of God, the celebration of this much-anticipated wedding feast, and the Lamb's rightful lordship over all the cosmos. Yet what we actually have in 19:11–21 is a gruesome description of *how* the Lamb ascends his throne.

What we may not quite expect, then, is the way the Lamb ascends his throne as John presents it in 19:11–21. The figure in 19:11–16 is never named as the Lamb or as Christ, but there can be no mistake that it is he. In 17:14 this particular battle is prophesied, and the Lamb conquers, for he is King of Kings and Lord of Lords. We have also seen the prophecy of the Lamb with his army on Mount Zion (chap. 14). Here in 19:16, the titles King of Kings and Lord of Lords are repeated of the heavenly Rider-Warrior. In an ingenious article, Monsignor Skeehan showed that, if the numerical values of the letters that spell these two titles in Aramaic are added together, they add up to 777. There can be no mistake that this king is goodness personified, the Lamb himself.

The heavenly Rider-Warrior comes forth to conquer in this final battle, prophesied in the sixth bowl (16:12–16); the "battle on the great day of God the Almighty" has arrived. Thus the battle fought in 19:17–21 is the eschatological battle at Armageddon foreshad-

106

owed in 16:16. The birds of prey that feed on carrion are gathered, so as to eat a "feast" on the flesh of the fallen. This is a gruesome way to describe the just judgment of those who worshiped the Beast. In the Old Testament, the wicked dead are often eaten by dogs as a just judgment, because it is a great dishonor deemed to be fitting for evildoers (e.g., Jezebel in 1 Kgs 21—22). The Beast and false prophet fall, and they are thrown into a sulfurous lake (brimstone). The fallen wicked are many; the birds are gorged. The King of Kings and Lord of Lords has slain the wicked with the sword of his mouth. This "feast" serves as an ironic negative counterpart to the wedding feast of the Lamb. Such irony is typical of Johannine literature; the staunch worshipers of the Beast prefer to *be* the feast rather than enjoy the heavenly banquet.

In 20:1–15 the events of the end continue. The last enemies of God and his people are finally destroyed. Satan is bound for a millennium before he too is thrown into the sulfurous lake. Thus the unholy parody of the Trinity is destroyed. There is also the last judgment, in which all the dead are judged according to their deeds, and death at last is also destroyed. With the conclusion of 20:15, therefore, there is the end of evil: it has at last been completely and irreversibly destroyed. Satan and his partners, as well as death and Hades (the realm of dead), are vanquished forever.

Questions

60. Is the entire revelation to John eschatological or just these last visions that begin at 19:11?
61. Why is Christ described as he is in 19:11–16?
62. What exactly is the lake of fire that burns with sulfur in 19:20; 20:10; and 20:14?
63. What is the meaning of Satan chained up for 1,000 years (20:2, 7)? How does it relate to the 1,000-year reign of Christ in 20:4–6?
64. What is the Rapture? Is it related to the *Parousia*, the Antichrist, and a great tribulation on earth at the end of the world?

65. What can be learned about the *eschaton* from the last-judgment scene in 20:11–15?

Conclusion

The Lamb's ascension to God's throne in heaven signifies his participation in God's almighty power and authority (12:5, anticipated in 11:17). The Lamb possesses all power and authority in the entire cosmos; he is truly Lord of all, then, including humanity. All things find their fulfillment in him, since he is the head of all creation and firstborn of the dead.

Christ dwells on earth in the midst of the Church (chap. 1). God's kingdom, therefore, is already present on earth in the Church, in an incipient fashion. With the "Christ event," God's kingdom is first established on earth, and his plan of salvation can be fulfilled. Revelation's septets tell the history of salvation and redemption, and the various expansions like interludes and appendices elaborate in showing that the ultimate fulfillment of this redemptive plan is happening now and coming imminently to consummation. The Church on earth lives in the end-times, and awaits the new creation, which includes the heavenly Jerusalem. The kingdom of God is manifested through the Church by her faithful and true witness to Jesus, by her signs (chap. 11 and 12), and also by her prophetic proclamation of the Gospel (chap. 10 and 11).

For John, the kingdom of God and of the Anointed One is already present on earth in the Church, but has yet to be brought to perfection. This reign of the Godhead is under attack by the forces of evil, and will be until the king returns in glory. By his death, resurrection, and ascension, Christ has definitely defeated evil, but by the Divine Will it has not yet been destroyed. In Johannine theology, Christ's death, resurrection, and ascension is his Passover, by which he, as the true Lamb, leads, as a new Moses, the new people of God into the heavenly promised land. Also brought into the kingdom are the repentant nations, who were not part of the earthly manifestation of the kingdom in the Church, but who as a result of the divine pedagogy of the septets have been made so by their conversion. John warns that those members of the churches who remain willfully unrepentant will not enter the heavenly kingdom.

Before the final consummation, the Church (the Two Witnesses and the Woman) undergoes persecution and trial. It is a time of distress, struggle, and vigilance for the Church. It is also, however, a time of prophetic witness that is characterized by the Spirit of Christ (19:10). The inhabitants of the earth and the worshipers of the Beast undergo distress as well, but this is during the same period of distress for the Church: the 1,260 days, 42 months, and the $3^1/_2$ years are all the same period of time. What has to be sorted out now at the end of human history is the wheat from the tare.

Thus, the true Passover Lamb brings a new exodus for his flock. The tyrant and his allies must first be defeated in order to liberate this new people of God. Into the promised land they will go, where they will with reign with him there as a covenanted kingdom of priests.

Section Fifteen:
Revelation 21:1—22:5

Introduction

This section is divided into two parts: the introduction, the announcement of God's eternal and covenantal dwelling with his faithful people, and the main portion, the Jerusalem Appendix (21:9—22:5). Together with the previous section, they comprise the eschatological visions (19:11—22:5).

Revelation 21:1–8 introduces the climactic eschatological vision of the new Jerusalem (21:9—22:5). After the three septets—the destruction of Babylon (18:1–24), final battle (19:11–21), and last judgment (20:1–15)—John's vision now moves to the goal of his entire apocalyptic-prophetic work: the new eschatological creation, with its center as the new Jerusalem (21:1—22:5).

With this vision of the new heaven and new earth, protology and eschatology meet. The first creation passes away so that it can be re-created (21:1). Like the Flood story in Genesis, the destruction of the world is God's opportunity for creating it anew, in short, for redeeming it. Unlike the Flood, in this re-creation there is no more evil, described here by the sea's existing no more. Re-creation in the *eschaton* is not exactly the same as in the beginning, but it is parallel, so that as a result the first creation of the cosmos serves as a type of the fulfilled eschatological reality to come.

Just as in the beginning, this eschatological re-creation is accompanied by salvation of a royal, priestly people. Unlike the covenant made through Moses, however, the covenant made through the Lamb is eternal. The language of 21:3 in which God dwells with his people echoes Old Testament covenant language (especially 2 Sam 7:14 and Ezek 37:23–27). As in the first covenant, God will dwell with his people in the new and ever-lasting covenant made in the Lamb's blood, making with them his "tent-tabernacle" (in Greek, *skēnoō;* 21:3; see also 7:15). In Old Testament terms, God will make his dwelling place (in Hebrew, *mishkan*) in the midst of his people.

Through the Old Testament prophets God promised an ever-lasting covenant that would keep his people from idolatry and sin and keep them faithful to him in their hearts. Ezekiel 37:23–27 speaks of that covenant, in which God will be their God and Israel will be his people. Revelation now envisions this promise and the promise to David (2 Sam 7) fulfilled. Revelation is making a deliberate wordplay with *skēnoō* and *mishkan*. *Mishkan,* dwelling place, is used of the tent of meeting in the wilderness (Exod 40), and of God's dwelling among his covenanted people (Ezek 37). From the same root is the Hebrew circumlocution for God, *shekinah*, which refers to his presence in the dwelling place, the tent of witness. John's audience would recognize the pregnant wordplay immediately. The wordplay cleverly expresses his theology of the new creation. It is the place where God's presence will dwell eternally with his faithful people, in a covenant that binds them to him forever, with no evil, suffering, or death.

In the heavenly Jerusalem, therefore, God will dwell with his royal, priestly people who will know his presence without media-tion. This new and eschatological salvation is modeled on the covenant made with Israel through Moses; the new exodus theme comes to its fullness here. God creates and redeems in the end-time in a manner similar to that at the beginning of salvation his-tory. The pattern is the same: creation, exodus-liberation, covenantal dwelling among his people. God's dwelling place, the home of his eternal presence and glory, is not a temple but his very own people, described in terms of a city (who is also the Bride; the imagery again pregnant with meaning). The eschato-logical salvation of God's covenanted people is described in 21:4 by an allusion to Isaiah 25:8 and 35:10, texts that speak of the salvation of a faithful remnant on the Lord's day; eschatological salvation has also been foreshadowed in the vision of the elect in chapter 7.

John sees God's dwelling as a holy city, which has already been identified as the Bride of the Lamb (21:2; 19:5–8), contrasted against the great Harlot, Babylon (21:9 and 17:1). The most natural way for the ancient biblical mindset to imagine the dwelling of God with his people is either in a temple or a city. John chooses the city so as to illustrate loyalty in terms of citizenship. Citizenship in the new Jerusalem is opposed to citizenship in the other womanly city, Babylon-Rome. In the heavenly Jerusalem the elect will no longer be strangers and sojourners or exiles and refugees: they will have eternal citizenship in the city where God dwells. Thus does Revelation's new exile theme come to its fullness here.

The description of God's dwelling among his people in the new Jerusalem, 21:9—22:5, is put, not just in terms of a city, but a *perfect* city; it is a flawless cube (21:16). The city is perfectly illuminated by God's glorious presence, depicted by brilliant and rare gems (21:11, 18–21; also chap. 4). In 21:18–20 there are pearly gates and streets paved with gold so pure they are like transparent glass. No expense is spared, as it were, in "building" a city fit for God's dwelling. This lavish splendor recalls the glory of the earthly Temple and city of Jerusalem, along with the high priest's breastplate, another allusion to the exodus (Exod 28:15–21).

The beauty and perfection of the heavenly city is like that of the earthly dwelling place for God in the first covenant, even though God's heavenly dwelling is more glorious than that of the tent of witness or Jerusalem's Temple. Relying on Ezekiel 40 to 48, John presents the heavenly Jerusalem as having twelve walls, gates, and names, and measuring to twelve squared. Clearly it is the home of the old and new Israel, represented by the twelve tribes and apostles both, and home of the 144,000 elect. The fact that the elect number twelve squared times 1,000, and that their heavenly homeland is composed of sets of twelve, is deliberate. By this John shows they belong here. A universal note is struck with three gates facing in each direction of the compass. The heavenly Jerusalem is described poetically so the reader can imagine it as well as desire to enter it. It is both splendid and fortified, the latter element a note of hope for a beleaguered Church.

Questions

66. What is the relationship of 21:1–8 to 19:1–8?
67. What is the relationship between the Bride of the Lamb, the heavenly Jerusalem, and the Woman clothed with the sun?
68. What is the meaning of the imagery used in 21:4 and 21:6?
69. What is the significance of the direct parallel between 17:1 and 21:9?
70. In 21:24 and 21:26, the glory and honor of the nations and kings are brought into the heavenly Jerusalem. Why?
71. Why is the imagery of a river and trees of life part of the description of the heavenly Jerusalem?

Conclusion

Twice we are told the holy city is from heaven and God (21:2, 10), a technique that helps recall the city is for the dwelling and communion of God with his priestly and royal people; it is God's dwelling "home" with humanity (21:3). The city gleams with God's very own splendor; the Bride shines with the Lamb's own light. This description of the heavenly city as a luminous place of God's glory is intentional; there is no temple in the city (21:22); it is illuminated by the Lamb, who is *Lychnos* (Greek for "lamp") to the seven *lychnia* (Greek literally for "little lamps," the diminutive of *lychnos*), that is, "Lamp to lamps" (21:23), a direct harking back to the seven lamp stands that symbolize the seven churches of chapters 1 to 3. The Church is *lychnia* and the One who stands in her midst is *Lychnos*. Thus, John nicely forms an inclusion with the opening visions of Revelation.

In the heavenly Jerusalem there is no mediated divine presence, only immediate communion between God and his people. There is no temple because the city itself is God's dwelling place, or, more precisely, the people are the place of his dwelling. Thus there is no need for a temple in God's eternal dwelling among humanity. But keeping with Revelation's multivalency (i.e., many symbols have multiple meanings), the faithful can rightly be described as permanent pillars in the temple because *they* will be God's eternal dwelling place (3:12); they *are* the temple. As in the Book of Exodus, God dwells with his covenanted people, but unlike the Mosaic covenant he dwells amidst his royal, priestly people without humanly constructed tent or temple or light. The heavenly Jerusalem, therefore, is not so much a place for redeemed people, but rather it is redeemed humanity as the place where God makes his home. The vision of the heavenly Jerusalem concludes with a scene of God and the Lamb enthroned, with the redeemed perpetually "serving" God. The heavenly Jerusalem is the eternal home of a priestly and royal people who participate in God's own kingship and priesthood by serving and reigning with him forever.

All of John's major themes and theologies come together in this climactic vision of God and the Lamb enthroned among the redeemed. This is the point toward which the whole narrative has been moving. God alone is king and those who worship him in fidelity will enjoy eternal covenantal union with him in his kingdom. The faithful take their rightful place in the perpetual liturgy (22:3), together with the four "living creatures," twenty-four elders, myriads of angels, and more. The faithful are marked with God's name on their foreheads. There is only goodness and truth and holiness in the vast assembly: there is nothing and no one profane, idolatrous, or deceitful. There is no trace of Satan or his allies. Death is no more; there is no one guarding the trees of life, for there is no need to do so. There is no darkness and no reason whatsoever to fear. There is only God in a new creation dwelling among his people in an eternal wedded union characterized by beatitude.

Review of Revelation 19:11—22:5

In this final section of the apocalypse proper, John presents visions of the "four last things." Revelation 19:11 and 4:1 are set in parallel by the verbal connector of "heaven opened." The two subdivisions of this main section are marked by similar phrasing in 11:19 and 15:5. The purpose of these divisions is to move the narrative forward while also defining their interrelationship.

The seals and trumpets come out of heaven, with John observing through the open door (4:1) as these visions concerning humanity's struggle to enter the kingdom of God begin. With 11:19, the temple of God in heaven is opened, the ark of the covenant is seen, and the triumph of the kingdom is announced. With each opening, John sees deeper into heaven, moving from the outside to the inner sanctum, so that as John enters further in, the narrative develops correspondingly. In 5:5 the tent of witness is opened and the conclusion of human history is poured out on the world. Finally, the Rider-Warrior (19:11) comes out of heaven to bring his people home and to perfect the consummation of the kingdom of God. These major subdivisions of the text indicate the narrative's movement, describing the overall situation of humanity and God's salvation of it by stages. The kingship of God and the Lamb are central themes throughout chapters 4 to 21, and here in 21 and 22, God enthroned is described as though John is not peeking through a doorway as in 4:1, but up close.

After having worked through the text of 19:11—22:5, some material in this section still needs further attention. It is perhaps easier to understand the function of the 1,000 years in chapter 20 if we think in terms of as two *simultaneous* millennia, one of Satan's binding and the other of the reign of the martyrs with Christ. (This idea is borrowed from R. Bauckham's *The Theology of the Book of Revelation,* 104–8; the rest of what is presented here is my own.)

The simultaneous millennia can be shown by John's own structure:

20:2–3	Satan is bound for 1,000 years so he will deceive the nations no more, until the 1,000 years are ended.
20:4	The martyrs reign with Christ 1,000 years.
20:5	The rest of the dead do not come to life until the 1,000 years are ended.
20:6	The martyrs reign with Christ 1,000 years.
20:7–8	Satan is released when the 1,000 years are ended so as to deceive the nations again.

The millennium of Satan consists of two parts: first, 20:2–3, in which Satan is bound until the 1,000 years are ended so as not to deceive the nations; and second, 20:7–8, in which Satan is released when the 1,000 years are ended, after which he deceives the nations once more. These two parts frame the millennium of the martyrs, which also consists of two parts: 20:4 and 20:6, in which the martyrs reign with Christ for 1,000 years; and 20:5, in which the rest of the dead do not rise until the 1,000 years are ended.

This last element tells us that the unmartyred dead do not return to life again until the 1,000 years are ended. The exact phrasing of "1,000 years are ended" is found only here and in the elements referring to Satan, while the reigning language is only found in those elements referring to the martyrs. Thus, there is an A:B:A:B:A pattern: A = 20:2–3; 20:5; and 20:7–8, respectively. B = 20:4 and 20:6, respectively. Though the general resurrection element of 20:5 is between 20:4 and 20:6, it has the same "1,000 years are ended" marker as the Satan elements. The millennium of the martyrs is thereby contrasted to that of Satan and the unmartyred dead. Accordingly, the contrast is between those who participate in the reign of Christ by virtue of already sharing in his resurrected life by their bloody witness of Jesus, with those who do not (the unmartyred dead and the nations). The martyrs live and reign during that 1,000 years, whereas the rest of the dead remain dead—they are bound too—while the nations are given the opportunity to convert before the end (20:8–10).

What can this structure tell us theologically? It seems clear that the 1,000 years of Satan's binding is in contrast to the 1,000 years of the reign of the martyrs. It is John's way of highlighting the martyrs' triumph over Satan in Christ. Their reign is characterized by enjoying the "first resurrection," that is, their triumph is complete and final; they have won. For them there is no fear of eternal damnation (the "second death"). Satan's binding, furthermore, is specifically in relation to the nations. While he is bound, his allies, the Beast and the false prophet, wreak havoc in his name (see chap. 12—13), attacking the Church, waging war against it, and making martyrs. This is the present evil age of persecution against the Church, described elsewhere as lasting 1,260 days or 42 months or $3^1/_2$ years. Recall that after the Dragon is defeated by God, he then wages war on the Woman's offspring, and immediately the Beast and the false prophet appear as his instruments. Christ (the "Stronger Man"; see Luke 11:20–22), by his death and resurrection, has bound Satan for this period in which the martyrs reign with him.

At the end of the age, that is, the consummation of human history, Satan will be loosed from his millennial binding, and turn to the nations who have been witnessed to and prophesied to by the Church during the 1,000 years. The point in the element about the nations not being deceived during the millennium is to show that in the end some will repent. Only after Satan is released is he allowed to deceive them. Thus 20:1–10 harks back to chapter 11, where the beloved city is trampled, the faithful are preserved, and the nations are prophesied and witnessed to. Verbal links here to chapters 11 and 12 are impressive: Ancient Serpent, deception, the casting from heaven and Satan's limitation or his binding, the only other mention of Jerusalem, and the depiction of the Church and the nations in battle. These verbal connections support this interpretation. In chapters 11 and 12 we also saw that the same period of time was identified by two different numbers, 1,260 days and 42 months, so as to emphasize the opposition of two groups. In a similar fashion, here the same number, 1,000, is used to highlight two different groups during the *same* period. So, there really are not two millennia, but one, told from the contrasting perspectives of the two opposing groups, Satan and the martyrs (so Bauckham).

Now the whole picture of this present evil age, which is eschatological and spans from the incarnation until the end of human history, comes together. Satan attacks the Woman but is thwarted; he is bound by Christ. In his place, his allies attack the Woman's offspring and the Two Witnesses. In the end, some from among the nations repent. The inhabitants of the earth do not. Those who are martyred for refusing to worship the Beast already share in the triumph of Christ, reigning with him. The millennium of the martyrs coincides with the millennium of Satan, but Satan's days are numbered: he will know the second death.

The first resurrection and the second death are metaphors; there are not literally two bodily resurrections or separations of soul from body. Those who enjoy the first resurrection must, therefore, also participate in the general resurrection (a second resurrection). Those who experience the first resurrection, as it were, do not, however, undergo the second death. The metaphors here are useful in conveying what the first resurrection is like: a participation in the resurrection of Christ starting in this earthly life that extends into eternal life in his kingdom, especially enjoyed by primary witnesses to Christ. Likewise, the second death (eternal damnation) is like the first one, only it is the reunited body and soul separated from God forever. These metaphors are an essential part of Johannine-realized eschatology.

Those who have eternal life cannot be harmed by the second death, and so they are blessed and holy indeed. The second resurrection does not guarantee that one avoids the second death, neither does the first death guarantee the first resurrection. John is encouraging Christians to witness to Jesus unto death. Eternal life is sometimes won that way. However, faithful Christians who do not suffer martyrdom may also gain eternal life, which is rewarded after the general resurrection and the last judgment. All the faithful and repentant—martyrs, Christians, and nations—will enjoy the kingdom of God and the eternal age of the Messiah, which is everlasting and atemporal and, therefore, has no corresponding numerical symbol.

The entire Book of Revelation is about the kingdom of God and the cosmic battle over humanity's soul. In this eschatological section, John highlights that those who bear witness to Jesus and the word of God, refusing to worship the Beast or compromise with the culture (i.e., accept its mark) already share in the reign of Christ, begun with his death-resurrection-ascension. The martyrs enjoy a special reward even beyond that; they also share in the judgment on their persecutors. Thus, their reward is emphasized and justice is finally given them (the fifth seal).

The same eschatological battle is told in both 19:17–21 and 20:7–11, foreshadowed by 16:12–16. John likes to recapitulate and enlarge. He has done so again here, depicting the final and definitive destruction of evil and God's enemies. The four last things are also shown here: Christ, as the heavenly Rider-Warrior, comes in glory (19:11) to judge (20:11). According to one's deeds, eternal life or damnation is given in the general last judgment, in which all the dead are raised up for judgment. The general resurrection is the second resurrection. The first death (body and soul separate) no one escapes; that is temporal. The second death (eternal damnation) is the unrepentant evildoer's just punishment and is not temporal. The first resurrection is the martyr's reward; the second resurrection no one escapes since it is part of the general last judgment and is universally essential: it is the restoration of the whole person, who then goes either to eternal life or death.

Since all will go in their entire persons, body and soul, judgment takes place only after all the dead are raised; likewise, what one did in the body is also judged. John emphasizes the first resurrection to say that individual Christians who persevere unto death (chap. 12) are especially blessed. Their place in the eternal kingdom of God is assured because their souls already share in it (20:4–6). The second death is for those who persecute the Church and oppose God, refusing to acknowledge his sovereignty, for those who worship the Beast, and for those who are still unrepentant. In the last judgment and general resurrection, some will go to life, some to death (Dan 12).

119

Revelation finishes with an extensive vision of the kingdom of God, the dwelling of God among his redeemed people. This people is priestly and royal, a people who serves God and participates in his reign. The dwelling of God among his people is in a new and eternal covenant. The blessedness of the elect as a people shepherded by the Lamb, living in his light and holiness forever, harks back to the portrayal of the elect in chapter 7. John expands the picture here, focusing on the divine dwelling and on the desire and reward of those who faithfully worshiped and bore witness to him in this world.

One of John's major themes, the holiness of God, is in the foreground in this section. It is God's holiness that is praised in worshiping him; he alone is worthy of worship because he alone is holy. This theme is a thread throughout 4:1—22:5 and is underscored in this last section, which is set in parallel to the scene of God's enthronement in chapters 4 and 5, with the two scenes forming bookends to the apocalypse proper. In the Old Testament, for the sake of his holy name among nations, God brings his people out of exile and settles back into their land. That is likewise the case here: God brings his people out of a new exile, into the heavenly promised land, where he dwells with them anew. This is, moreover, an eternal covenant (see Jer 31; Ezek 34), made in the blood of the Lamb. God's people are finally cleansed of idolatry and impure worship, and the Davidic Shepherd rules them (Ezek 38).

The new exodus theme is unmistakably prominent in this section as well: God has delivered his people from the tyrant, bringing them by the blood of the Lamb through the Red Sea to himself in the new promised land of the heavenly Jerusalem. It is here he dwells among them as their God, they as his people. In this eternal covenant they are espoused to him forever, as his Bride. Salvation for God's people in a renewed promised land is finally fulfilled.

Lastly, there is a good deal of typical Johannine symbolism here in chapters 21 and 22, for example, light/darkness, water/spirit. The use of such symbolism in this section highlights the splendor and glory of the heavenly Jerusalem: there is only the light of God, no darkness of Satan. There is no desert of temptation and wandering, but only the water of life that is the Spirit.

As we saw, Revelation contains many visions of divine chastisement and wrath, particularly in the three septets of the seals (6:1— 8:2), trumpets (8:2—11:18), and bowls (15:5—16:21), the overall purpose of which is to encourage repentance and conversion while there is still time, as God prepares his people for the final consummation of his kingdom. Revelation's theology of an imminent consummation of all things (1:1–3; 11:18; 22:7, 10, 12, 20) expresses the great urgency of its proclamation of the eternal Gospel to the whole world (14:6). Because there is no more delay (10:6–7), sinners—sinful Christians and idolaters alike—must accept that Good News and repent now, and the Church is again commissioned to preach it (10:7, 8–11; 11:3).

Revelation's urgent tone is not meant to inspire in the sinner dread and fear, but sincere conversion and the desire for divine mercy. God's chastisements are meant to bring conversion, not condemnation, as can be seen in 9:4–5, 20–21; 11:13 (where it works) and 16:9, 11 (where it does not work). "Fear God and give him glory" (11:13; 16:9) is an Old Testament expression that refers to the conversion of pagans to the Living God, shown especially in worship and praise of him and the forsaking of idols. Although God's long-suffering toward sinners causes the Church more suffering (6:9–11), it also gives the Church an opportunity to participate in the Lamb's redemptive sacrifice.

In the septets of the seals and trumpets, it becomes clear with the one-quarter and the one-third destructions (6:8; 8:7) that these plagues are meant to teach repentance and conversion rather than to punish. There is a divine pedagogy. The final plagues (the bowls) are meant to do so as well, though they also act as a divine punishment of the unrepentant because they are total (16:1–9) and final (15:1; 16:17). A close reading will show that the final plagues are one of the book's few punishments of unrepentant sinners (11:13; 18:20; 19:2). That such divine punishment appears comparatively little in Revelation, and only so strikingly as late as the third and final septet, betrays the book's overriding concern for salvation and mercy for the sinner.

To this punishment the unrepentant simply blaspheme, which is emphasized by its being mentioned twice (16:9, 11). This blasphemy demonstrates God's justice in punishing the unrepentant after repeated attempts to teach them repentance. It is noteworthy that only after the final plagues are finished is the divine judgment on unrepentant sinners carried out: the last battle (19:11–21) and judgment (20:1–15) are not punishments but strictly eschatological and universal events carried out at the end of human history, after the possibility for repentance is over. Thus are God's divine forbearance and patience portrayed by these three septets, which comprise a large portion of the apocalyptic visions (4:1—22:5), and which most readers wrongly take to be severe judgments on all humanity by an arbitrarily wrathful god. The divine long-suffering and the perpetual mercy toward sinners is a major theme of Revelation, which has at its core the hope for universal salvation and concern for sincere conversion.

REVELATION
22:6–21

Introduction

This final section is Revelation's epilogue, which contains many parallels to the prologue and introduction. Note once again the book's letter format: the epistolary conclusion in the epilogue (22:21) is parallel to the epistolary greeting in 1:4–6. There are other verbal connections between Revelation's opening and closing sections (1:1, 19 and 22:6; 1:3 and 22:7; 1:9 and 22:8 and 1:3, 9 and 22:9, 18). In the epilogue, John makes his final exhortation for fidelity to Christ by emphasizing that the Lord is coming soon. There, Christ himself speaks three times of his coming as imminent (22:7, 12, 20).

In this final exhortation, Christ promises that when he comes he will reward each as his conduct deserves (22:12); his judgment is not arbitrary (20:11–13). In 22:13, it is Christ who speaks of himself as the Alpha and Omega, though we have also seen the same title used of God in 1:8 and 21:6. This indicates that Christ shares in the ontological prerogatives of God the Father and not just in his reign. By means of these titles, which are allusions to Old Testament texts, John frames his vision in a way that underscores its source and authenticity.

The beatitude in 22:14 again uses the image of washing robes so as to obtain eternal life. As in 7:14, Christ's redemptive sacrifice is the only way to enter the kingdom (1:5; 12:11). The images of the tree of life, and of the thief who enters by climbing the walls, recall the expulsion from paradise, connecting eschatology with protology yet again. It is also a pastoral image (John 10). By his own testimony that the entire revelation is true, Christ reminds the churches of their relationship to him and recalls the letters to them. He is the Messiah (22:16b; also 2:26–27; 5:5) and promises them his abiding presence eternally if they are worthy (2:28; 22:14).

In 22:17, the Spirit and the Bride say "come." The Spirit and Church (Bride) of Christ both long for Christ's Second Advent and the consummation of the kingdom he will bring with it. His warning in 22:18 to "everyone who hears" is like his "Let anyone who has an ear listen to what the Spirit is saying to the churches" in the seven letters (e.g., 3:6). It is an urgent exhortation to the faithful. Thus the Spirit and the Church are connected in both the letters and the epilogue; anyone who has ears heeds what the Spirit says, and as members of the Church, the faithful can heed and pray together with the Spirit for the Bridegroom to "come."

The final prophetic exhortation of the epilogue, taken in conjunction with the initial prophetic exhortation of chapters 1 to 3, highlights the fact that the people of God *are judged as individuals, but saved as a people.* The invitation from Christ in 22:17b to be shepherded recalls 7:15–17 and reflects a longing by the Church for the messianic kingdom. Revelation 22:20b is the liturgical cry of the Church in response to "The Witness" (22:20a; "the *one* who testifies"), which is one of the most important titles of Christ in this work, as well as being the first and last used of him (1:5). The Witness's last words to his Bride are a promise of his imminent Advent. The liturgical response by the Church's assembly—"Amen. Come, Lord Jesus"—indicates that it welcomes that Advent and prays longingly for it.

The reminder in 22:12, 20 of the Bridegroom's imminent Advent is not intended to frighten but to encourage: the coming of Christ in glory is to save his Bride, to bring her into his dwelling forever. Note the use once again of God's oft-repeated title in Revelation; "Who is and who was and who is to come." Recall that it is not "who *will* be" because John is more concerned with God's coming to save than with his ontological reality. Thus the final exhortation of the epilogue encourages God's people to prepare for the Lord's coming to save them by his bringing the kingdom to its ultimate consummation.

Questions

72. What is the point of not sealing up the book (22:10)?
73. What are the various indications that John understands this work as prophecy?
74. Why does the list of "outsiders" in 22:15 include dogs among the evildoers?
75. It is striking that in the end of the book, Jesus finally addresses the reader directly (22:16–20). What can be learned from this?
76. "Amen. Come, Lord Jesus!" Why is this an appropriate response to the final testimony in this book?
77. In what way is Revelation a fitting conclusion to the New Testament?

Conclusion

Basically the book tells the story of the final triumph of God in Christ, in which evil is finally and completely vanquished and the kingdom consummated in full at long last. The overall purpose of the book is to encourage the people of God who are suffering persecution and distress for their faithful witness to Jesus and the word of God.

Revealed in the visions of each section of the book and in the septets (recapitulated, each time with sharper focus and expansion) is that suffering in Christ serves God's purposes, especially in routing out evil. For the faithful in particular, suffering has meaning because it may result in their own patient endurance and participation in bearing the witness of Jesus. For Revelation, as with much of the New Testament, suffering is actually a necessary and salvific element of God's plan for the world's salvation (e.g., Mark 8:31; John 3:16). What John does differently here from most of the New Testament authors is depict the Church's part in Christ's suffering rather than Christ's own passion and death. (Though in this, of course, Revelation is similar to Acts, albeit in a different genre and imperial period.) The Church thereby continues the redemptive work of Christ on earth. The emphasis is that the suffering of the faithful is not in vain; its positive result is the repentance of the nations and the long-awaited accomplishment of divine justice.

In Revelation, John warns the Church not to conform to this world, which worships the Beast and is hostile to God. John's hope is that the Church will help to bring the ungodly to worship the true God. This prophetic exhortation is part of John's general overall encouragement for Christians to endure patiently in, with, and through Christ, that is, to be willing to "wash their robes in the blood of the Lamb." God's fidelity to his people is revealed in a terribly dramatic way in John's vision; his people are called to wait hopefully for him to act.

The suffering of the unfaithful is intended by God to have good effects as well as to punish, that is, the overall role of their suffering in the book is to bring them to conversion, and then ultimately to salvation. The faithful suffer in order to bring in the unfaithful, and the ungodly suffer so as to be moved to repent. Distress is one of God's chief pedagogical tools for learning the way of salvation.

Suffering is a means of chastisement, punishment, and justice, but it can also be redemptive. Indeed, the shedding of the Lamb's blood on the cross is the primary proof and means of this. God's will is mysteriously accomplished in the suffering of all people, godly and ungodly. The suffering of both the faithful and the unfaithful points to God's merciful patience, and the endurance of the saints he richly rewards. Distress patiently endured in Jesus results in a proleptic sharing in his reign, in hope of full participation in the kingdom where the One Enthroned and the Lamb are perpetually worshiped for all eternity, and only goodness and beatitude are known.

Review of Revelation 22:6–21

A main concern of the author of the book is the struggle between good and evil, depicted symbolically in terms that were understandable and significant to his contemporary audience. God and the Lamb battle the Dragon and his allies, with the Church between them. The battle between the Church and the Roman Empire mirrors this supernatural battle between God and Satan. Thus, for John the seer, there are two levels of reality, the heavenly and the earthly. One is reflected in the other, with the primary and important reality being the heavenly one. John seeks to make sense of the suffering of the faithful as he narrates this cosmic battle.

The expectation of God's imminent, definitive intervention on behalf of his people, which will result in the dual effect of the defeat of Satan and the final consummation of the kingdom of God, is based on the Paschal Mystery. Since the victory of the cross has already been won, Satan's days are limited. So, attacks on the Church are not to last; Satan is already defeated. And yet, Satan has not yet been completely vanquished. The war is won although it is still being waged. Once Satan is completely vanquished, there will be a new world, the kingdom of God and the Lamb, where God will be worshiped and his sovereignty acknowledged and praised by all creation. The faithful will have everlasting life and bliss in his presence, dwelling with him as a covenanted bride. Thus, God, the Lord of History and Creation, who is worthy of all worship, really is in control of the universe, though it may not seem so to a beleaguered Church. Soon, when Christ comes again, God will be recognizably in control, and Satan powerless.

John seeks to console his fellow sufferers, encouraging them to wait and endure patiently, standing fast in their witness to the Word of God until he comes. The epilogue highlights Jesus' promise to come soon. There is an urgent exhortation in this concluding section to act in faith and to hope that what the Lord has promised is trustworthy and absolutely reliable. There is also a prayerful expectation that those who remain faithful will share in the triumph of the Lamb forever.

Though the narrative is contextualized in Asia Minor of the late first century, its theology is timeless and universal. All of humanity encounters evil and suffering. Our temporal condition is marked by a constant struggle with suffering and distress. The book seeks to put this daily struggle in context: John's perspective is that all of the cosmos is in fact involved in an intense battle between good and evil. What John attempts to do, therefore, is to relate the outcome of this cosmic battle and thereby assure the faithful that the triumph of good is certain (1:1; 4:1; 22:6). He knows this because it has been revealed to him by the Redeemer himself, who will ride forth yet again to vanquish forever the enemies of God and his people.

John recognizes the dreadful reality of evil; he and his fellow servants of God suffer distress from the continual onslaught of the power and servants of Satan. His purpose is to encourage the people of God in the face of this evil as they await the final consummation of the kingdom, which is relevant to the Church of every age; for with the incarnation, the eschatological era dawned. For John, evil is neither to be ignored nor to be blindly submitted to by the Christian. Rather, it is to be faced and overcome in Christ, whether by the patient endurance of the suffering that it brings or otherwise "bearing the witness of Jesus."

According to John's theological outlook, evil is part of reality and is inescapable until this temporal order passes away. John understands that patient endurance of distress in Christ transforms the sufferer into a victor who shares in Christ's own triumphant reign, even in this fallen world. The faithful Christian participates in helping to bring the final consummation of the kingdom by such virtuous activity, which enables the sufferer to transcend the world's futility and deception of sin and infidelity to the Creator. A faithful servant is conformed to Christ, not to evil.

How is it that patient endurance in Christ overcomes evil, aids in establishing the kingdom, and transcends futility and deceit? If evil brings suffering and distress, why is it apparently destroyed only by suffering and distress? For John the answer to this paradox lies in the mystery of the incarnation: in God's mysterious plan of salvation, evil is conquered only by the cross of Christ. Christ's suffering and death are the sole means of redemption, and so it is only in him and in his blood that suffering has any meaning or good effect at all. In other words, the power to save from evil, as well as to destroy it, comes from the blood of the Lamb (1:5–6; 5:9–10). Christians' imitation of Christ and union with him in suffering bring participation in this life-giving, liberating power (7:14; 12:10–11). The cross and resurrection of Christ inaugurate his reign; the suffering and death of the saints play an essential part in bringing it to completion.

According to the book, the Church's distress is an opportunity for sharing in Christ's death, which brings a corresponding sharing in his life. Distress happens to others besides the faithful. In a real way, the book's presentation of distress is universal, since plagues fall on the good and bad alike, and both negative and positive responses to the distress are made. Furthermore, John demonstrates in his visions that all distress is either actively permitted or inflicted by God. The septets of the seals, trumpets, and bowls make that especially clear, albeit in a violent fashion. John's theology of distress and suffering, in all its dimensions, is unveiled when these three septets of chapters 4 to 22 are examined in the context of the consummation of the kingdom as the final triumph of good over evil. The patient endurance of the faithful in Christ, which the entire Book of Revelation seeks to encourage, is situated within the context of the eschatological distress in which the kingdom is already present and by which it is finally brought to perfection.

Answers

Section One:
Revelation 1:1–20

1. The title to this last book of the New Testament comes from its first verse, which says that it is a "revelation of Jesus Christ." In the original Greek, the word for *revelation* is *apokalypsis*. It is from this word that a whole body of literature gets its name: from 200 BC to AD 200 there were many "apocalypses" written; the Apocalypse of John (or Book of Revelation) was only one of them. What is characteristic of this literature is that the author-seer claims to have been given a Revelation by God, that is, that God has unveiled something hidden to him. The Apocalypse of John claims to be a revelation from and about Jesus Christ. It is a single Revelation comprised of many visions.

   Currently in America, when someone hears the word *apocalypse,* they think of the term's common meaning as it is popularly used, namely, to mean the final conflagration of the world (*Armageddon* is usually part of it). However, in actuality, the apocalypse refers to the last book of the New Testament, a piece of literature, not an event. Thus the apocalypse is not an event at the end of the world, but the last book of the Bible, which is called the Book of Revelation or the Apocalypse of St. John.

   Many people often mistakenly refer to it as "Revelations." While there are many visions and series of visions in this work, there is *only one revelation* in the Apocalypse of St. John, that of Jesus Christ to John (1:1). The Latin from which we derive the English title of this book, *revelatio,* is singular, and it is a translation from the original Greek title of the book, *apokalypsis,* which is also singular. So the actual text of the Book of Revelation calls itself *an* apocalypse, or *a* revelation, not revelations.

2. Beginning in chapter 1 and throughout the book, John the seer claims to have many visions. This is not just a literary device to relate the book's theology in manageable sections. It is also a typical part of biblical prophecy. Like Ezekiel or Isaiah in the Old Testament, John is a biblical prophet who is granted visions from God. In the Bible God often communicates with his prophets in this way. They in turn relate and interpret the visions in order to deliver God's word to his people in a compelling way. In ancient Israel, the use of prophecy thrived for a long time, and then died out. In the New Testament era, it was reborn for a time; Revelation is one example of it.

3. The author of the Book of Revelation, or the Apocalypse, calls himself John. The fact that he gives no further hint as to his identity implies that he is so well known among the early Christians of the province of Asia Minor, he doesn't have to do so. Christian tradition has overwhelmingly identified John as the son of Zebedee, one of the twelve apostles and the evangelist of the Fourth Gospel. Also according to tradition, the apostle John was exiled to Patmos by Domitian when that emperor's attempt to boil him alive in oil failed due to divine intervention; the bath seemed to John like a comfortable rejuvenating one. Patmos was a Roman penal colony, and it was there that the book is said to have been written. John may be reticent to identify himself as an apostle since he is writing under persecution, but also because he clearly sees this work as a prophecy.

4. The reader will discover that throughout this book there is a good deal of liturgical language and symbolism. We tend to forget that the original context of much of the New Testament was the liturgy. Letters or Gospels would be read in the liturgical assembly on the Lord's day (Sunday), when Christians gathered for communal worship. John seems to intend his apocalypse to be distributed and read in such a context. John also wishes to convey the idea that God is worthy of ceaseless praise from all of creation, and

so he expresses much of his theology in liturgical language. In addition, hymns are often used in Revelation to elaborate on or interpret a scene or vision.

5. Christ is depicted as the king (or emperor) of the universe in language and images taken primarily from the Old Testament. For example, God (the Father) is often described in terms of fire or light. In transferring these descriptions from God the Father to Christ the Son, John subtly and unmistakably makes the point that Christ is also divine, sharing in God's power and glory. For us these descriptions may be unfamiliar or foreign, but to the early Christians they would be very familiar and easily grasped. The descriptions make the point that he is the true ruler and, therefore, will take care of his faithful subjects, and that Domitian is a fraud who has wrongfully claimed to rule the universe.

6. Throughout the book the expression "testimony (witness) of Jesus Christ" appears often, and usually together with "testimony (witness) to the word of God." The Greek word translated by testimony or witness is the root word from which we get *martyr*. Christians who bear ultimate witness to Christ by giving up their lives are martyrs; others may also bear witness though not unto death. This testimony and witness have Christ both as their origin and goal. Christ is also the Word of God, as is scripture. John and other early Christians would have testified by their faith and their lives to Christ and his holy word.

Section Two:
Revelation 2:1—3:22

7. John envisions the Church in a cosmic battle between good and evil, and so he depicts the Christian life in terms of spiritual warfare (cf. Eph 6). This is typical of apocalyptic litera-

ture and of much of the Jewish and Christian writing of John's time. The Christian is called to share in Christ's victory over sin, evil, and ultimately death, but to do so the Christian disciple must conquer sin, vice, and evil. In each letter, Christ promises to those who conquer—that is, those who persevere in fidelity to him and the Gospel—that they will share his life in heaven forever.

Christ is presented in Revelation 1 as the risen and triumphant Son of Man. He is, like many a Roman emperor, a true conquering hero. He has vanquished his enemies—sin, death, and Satan—and now reigns, exalted and glorious. Christians who faithfully follow him also share in that reign even now in this world (1:9). In these seven letters, Christ promises his faithful disciples that they will share in his reign forever, a great encouragement to disenfranchised Christians. Like other New Testament authors, John draws from life in the Roman empire of his day to speak of life in Christ.

8. The strange names in the seven letters are best understood to be persons or groups who are opposed to the Church or who represent various factions within the local church communities that are stirring up trouble or leading people astray. The Nicolaitans are not mentioned anywhere except in these letters; they appear to be Christians who compromised their faith by continuing in certain pagan practices. Balaam and Jezebel are symbolic names, taken from the Old Testament (Num 22—24; 1 Kgs 17—21, respectively). Both these people were considered foreigners who led Israel astray; here they are probably leading members of the various local churches into serious sin by compromising with the pagan culture. Antipas is clearly a martyr about whom we know only what is said here (Rev 2:13).

As for expressions like "Satan's synagogue-throne" or even where he dwells, they point to a polemic between Christians and Jews in John's day. In this particular era, Jews made accusations against Christians to the authorities that resulted in their arrest, and often also their execution (like Polycarp of Smyrna or Ignatius of Antioch). Since in Hebrew *Satan* means "the accuser," it is a play on words to identify those who accuse Christians, in this case the members of the local synagogue, as in league with him. John is not being anti-Jewish (he himself is a Palestinian Jew); rather, he thinks so highly of Jews, as is evidenced in 3:9, that he says Christians are the authentic Jews because they have accepted Christ. Moreover, John is not singling out the Jews here: the term *Satan's throne* is likewise used in 2:13 to refer to the center of pagan worship and the cult of the emperor. Thus, for John, anyone who persecutes the Church is an instrument of Satan.

9. It is rarely more clear than in this expression that John is a biblical prophet. Compare similar sayings by Jesus (e.g., Matt 13:9; Luke 8:8). The expression is a challenge and invitation to pay attention and heed what the Spirit is telling the churches. It is an admonition to repent and be faithful. It is also directed to individual churches, as well as to the whole Church, because in each letter the saying is repeated to all seven churches. As with other biblical prophets, the Spirit is speaking through the prophet what God wishes his people to hear.

10. Like the letters of St. Paul addressed to various local churches, these seven letters contain references to specific details that are part of the makeup of daily life in that era. Many of these details are obscure to us because they presume intimate knowledge of the communities that we do not share. One wonders perhaps why they are included in this work, since they are so parochial. Yet they are pertinent to the universal Church and serve as an exhortation for Christ's disciples to follow him in the concrete circumstances and vicissitudes of daily life. In every age there are still factions in local churches, or heterodox teachers, or persecution, and there is still the temptation for the individual Christian as well as the community to conform to the world and the culture rather than to Christ and his

Gospel. The particulars of these letters, including their exhortations, admonitions, and praises, may help Christians of every age remember that Christianity is lived in the concrete circumstances of daily life and is not simply a matter of intellectual assent to a set of doctrine.

Section Three: Revelation 4:1–11

11. What happens to the seer in chapter 4 is also typical of Old Testament prophecy. The prophet Ezekiel, for example, is described in ecstasy or transported in the spirit (e.g., Ezek 1 and 37). What such prophets describe seems to be an intense mystical experience. St. Paul also claims to have had such an experience (2 Cor 12). The biblical prophets were powerfully inspired by the Spirit; this was constitutive of God's delivering his word to his people through them.

12. John describes God enthroned in heaven in ways that seem fantastic and unreal. Yet, he is simply continuing the tradition of the great biblical prophets like Ezekiel and Isaiah before him; compare Ezekiel 1 and 2 and Isaiah 6 to this scene, noting how similar they are. Like the Old Testament prophets before him, John describes the glory of the Lord without ever really describing him, the invisible and transcendent God. But John's description conveys God's reality: he dwells in light refulgent; he is perpetual light, luminous and brilliant like gems. It is appropriate to have cosmic signs like thunder, lightening, and earthquakes to describe his almighty presence, reminiscent of Sinai (Exod 19). Kings are splendid and wealthy; thus God is described in earthly equivalents like light and gems.

   John is using Old Testament imagery to describe God so that the reader familiar with the Old Testament will immediately recognize the One Enthroned in chapter 4 as God the Father. Because John uses the same imagery to describe

God as the Old Testament books of Exodus, Ezekiel, and Isaiah, the reader with a good knowledge of Old Testament thought can begin to recognize here that John is also thereby presenting two motifs that will occur throughout his work, namely, the exodus and the exile. Two of John's major themes in Revelation 4:1—22:5 is a new exodus and a new exile for the new people of God (the Christians, or the Church), because they are really strangers in captivity in this world who require liberating.

Recall that the Book of Exodus tells the story of the exodus of the original people of God by signs and wonders. Ezekiel begins his prophecy in Babylon among the exiled people of God, and Isaiah prophesies a return from exile using new-exodus imagery. John uses imagery from these books to strike the same themes, except not in relation to the Israelites, the ethnic Jews, but rather to the "true children of Abraham" (in John's thinking), the Christians. Christians suffering persecution and martyrdom would be encouraged by new-exodus language, hoping for God to save them from oppression and bring them to himself where they will live freely with him in an everlasting covenant. Christians of the late New Testament era certainly saw themselves as strangers in exile (see 1 Pet). Reaching the heavenly kingdom of God would be equivalent to a return from exile to one's homeland.

13. John describes here some members of the heavenly court, particularly twenty-four elders, and four "living creatures" who are tetramorphs (four-shaped). The elders are seated on thrones, dressed in white robes and wearing golden crowns, which they take off when falling down in homage before God, whom they worship perpetually. Because there are twenty-four of them, most scholars understand these elders to be angelic representatives of the people of God, both old and new. The Israelites had twelve tribes and the new Israel (the Church) has twelve apostles (who were promised to sit on thrones in heaven; see Luke 22:30). Twelve plus twelve makes twenty-four, so that the number

of elders is the sum of God's old and new people. In this interpretation the function of these elders is to offer adoration to God on behalf of humanity, represented by his old and new covenanted people.

However, in another interpretation, the elders are priests of the new creation. The Old Testament temple had twenty-four courses of priests to serve the Lord. Since there is no indication in the text that twenty-four is to be obtained by adding twelve plus twelve, and also because they are all the same (rather than two different sets of twelve), this interpretation is plausible. What makes it more attractive is that they appear to be royal priests: they are dressed in white robes with gold crowns. Given the context of their appearance, namely, service of God in perpetual worship, it makes sense that they are priests, especially given the strong emphasis on worship here.

The four "living creatures" are certainly bizarre. They are, however, very similar to the angels described in Ezekiel's and Isaiah's inaugural visions (Ezek 1 and Isa 6). Their purpose is to offer praise and worship to God ceaselessly. Four is often symbolic of the cosmos or the whole of creation in biblical thought, much as it is in modern thinking (e.g., four points of the compass, or the "four winds"). So, the four "living creatures" may represent all of creation before God. In Christian tradition they have been interpreted as the four Gospels or evangelists. Irenaeus said that the lion was Mark, the ox was Luke, the human face was Matthew, and the eagle in flight was John (*Against Heresies* III.ix.8). In his commentary on Ezekiel, Jerome said the lion was John and the eagle Mark (*Hiezechielem* I.i.6/8), with the other two the same as Irenaeus' reckoning. In this thinking the four "living creatures" may represent the fourfold Gospel as it is preached throughout creation, from men and women, and even to the birds. In any case, these four "living creatures" are angels made by God to stand before his throne in endless praise.

140

Section Four:
Revelation 5:1–14

14. The scroll (*biblion* in Greek) given by God to the Lamb is meant to be mysterious: it is perfectly sealed and unusual in itself, and can be opened only by one who is worthy. These elements of the scroll help to interpret what it is. In antiquity a scroll would have been written on only one side. That this one is written on both sides indicates its uniqueness and that it has much in it to be revealed. It contains divine proclamations that will be unveiled only by the Lamb, who alone is worthy to announce the scroll's content.

    The seven seals have to be opened before the scroll can be read, and so the reader knows to expect that. Given what happens starting in chapter 6 with the breaking of the seven seals, the best interpretation of the scroll is that it is God's plan of salvation. This makes even better sense when combined with the declaration that only the Lamb is worthy to open it. Christ alone in all the universe can carry out the divine plan of salvation because he alone is worthy by virtue of his death and resurrection. Christ is, moreover, not just the Redeemer but also the Revelation of God, his Word, and so the one most appropriate to reveal God's word contained in the scroll. The Lamb's acceptance of the scroll indicates his acceptance of this commissioning. Some interpreters understand the scroll to be the Old Testament, but that is probably not the best reading, although clearly Christ does fulfill the Old Testament as part of God's salvific plan. Thus, to say it is the Old Testament is not really specific or inclusive enough, especially since the Old Testament is not a sealed book in any sense.

15. It is logical that Revelation should speak of Christ as a Lamb. John the Baptist heralds him as the "Lamb of God" (John 1), and in the Fourth Gospel, John the evangelist presents Jesus as the true Passover Lamb. It is typical of apocalyptic literature to use animals (like "living creatures"

or beasts) to represent kingdoms or empires similar to using an elephant, donkey, or bear to represent a nation or a significant national group. Daniel 7 to 12 uses, among other creatures, a ram, or adult male sheep. Does John envision here a ram or a year-old male lamb? Both? It is hard to imagine he does not at least envision something like the wild ram indigenous to Palestine. It is likewise difficult to say John does not also envision a sacrificial lamb as well.

Revelation often uses language from Exodus, and, like the Fourth Gospel, a Passover Lamb would fit here. If Christ is the Passover Lamb here as well, the point is much the same as that in John's Gospel: Christ liberates God's people from sin, death, and evil. The tyrant, in this case Domitian and not Pharaoh, will not ultimately triumph. The blood of the Passover Lamb saves Israel, and the blood of Christ saves all humanity. Christ as the new Passover Lamb is sacrificed to bring salvation. Thus he was slaughtered but now lives again. No Christian could hear such a description and not know immediately that it is Christ (much as every Christian knows immediately who Aslan is, when they read C. S. Lewis's *Chronicles of Narnia*). This description helps the reader to focus on Christ as Redeemer; it is the crucified and risen one who saves. The Lamb won the right to carry out the universal divine plan of salvation because of his victory on the cross (Rev 5:5).

The Lamb who was slaughtered but now lives, "a Lamb standing as if it had been slaughtered," has seven eyes and seven horns. This description is not meant to be taken literally but as a metaphorical way of suggesting certain things about Christ. He is omniscient and almighty. He is also the Lion of the tribe of Judah, the Root of David. These two images are messianic ones drawn from the Old Testament (see Gen 49:9 and Isa 11:10); the Lamb is none other than the Messiah, but not literally a lamb, a lion, or a root. Taken all together the description of Christ here conveys consolation and encouragement to the suffering faithful: Christ is the Sacrificial Lamb that effects salvation. He can carry out the divine plan entrusted to him because by his once-for-all sacrifice he won the right to do so. He is the Messiah who reigns over God's kingdom, and so he is aptly described as the Lion of Judah and as the Root of Jesse (cf. Isa 11). Because he is all-seeing, he knows what the faithful need. Because he is almighty, he will triumph on behalf of his faithful and bring them into his kingdom.

16. Throughout Revelation there are many symbolic numbers, with seven being by far the most frequent. Seven is used in the biblical mindset to represent perfection and fullness. For example, God rested on the seventh day (Gen 1). So the scroll is completely, perfectly sealed if it has seven seals. The Lamb is omniscient because he has seven eyes; he is almighty because he has seven horns (the horns of a ram or any large animal are powerful and deadly, and so they represent power; cf. Dan 7—12). There is a series of septets (visions with seven elements) in Revelation: seven letters, seven seals, seven trumpets, and seven bowls.

17. Hymns help to interpret what is happening. That is the case here whenever there is a new song sung. There is a new hymn when God is doing something new, that is, when he is implementing a new phase of salvation history. In this instance it is because the Lamb has accepted his role in carrying out the divine plan of salvation. The crucified and risen Christ will now complete God's work of redemption. The emphasis of the new hymn in 5:9–10 is the new covenant made in the blood of the Lamb. By his death, Christ makes a new covenant in his blood. The language of the new hymn is very much like that of Exodus 19:6, in the making of the first covenant. The idea here is that, in Christ, God has made a new people for himself, this time not through the sacrifice of *a* lamb but through the sacrifice of *the* Lamb; this time not just from one ethnic group (Jews by birth), but from "every tribe and language and people and nation." The Israelites were to be a kingdom of

priests, or a royal priesthood, that is, a people who served and worshiped God alone. In Revelation, the Church is the new Israel, and this new Israel, like the old, is a royal priesthood set apart for God alone.

Now, therefore, when the Lamb receives the scroll, the heavenly court praises God for this new thing he has wrought. Not only is God Creator and Sovereign over all things, he is Lord of History: in Christ, history finds its fulfillment and consummation. God's providential care of all is then lauded by the twenty-four elders, the four "living creatures," myriads and myriads of angels, and, in fact, by all of creation.

Section Five: Revelation 6:1–17

18. One of the chief literary characteristics of apocalypses, and John's is certainly a good example, is the extensive use of symbolism. Colors, numbers, animals, cosmic imagery, and the like are all part of the literary makeup of apocalypses. It seems to have been constitutive of the apocalyptic mindset in the same way, perhaps, that various artists (poets, painters, etc.) have a language in which to express their views of the world, which are neither prosaic nor conventional. The apocalyptic mindset understood that humanity is caught in a cosmic battle between good and evil, and that its ultimate resolution is possible only with divine intervention and the end of the world.

Another reason for the apparently "covert language" is that apocalypses were generally authored by persons and addressed to communities suffering persecution for religious reasons. The covert language would be easily understood by those communities, who shared the world vision and symbolic arsenal of the author, but not by the oppressors. The pagan Romans who persecuted the early Christian Church certainly did not understand symbolism like lions and lambs, rooted in the Old Testament. Covert language avoids further trouble from oppressors; apocalypses are a form of underground resistance literature.

But the rhetoric of apocalypses is not to be underestimated. One of the things John wants to do with his symbolism and imagery is to motivate his readers to be faithful, to take courage, and to withstand persecution. The way he relates his visions and the way he tells the story of this cosmic battle are meant to move his audience to behave in certain ways. Emotions and attitudes are evoked and stoked by John's symbolism, in much the same way poetry or music moves us. The best way to move John's beleaguered audience is by shaping his theology in visions that tell a story, rather than in an intellectual treatise. The visions, together with their meaning, will be both grasped and remembered by his audience far better than any philosophical discourse or exhortatory sermon might be.

It is also the case that the symbolism and imagery of this book are part of what makes it so intriguing and memorable. John's vision may not have been preserved had it been a plain and simple piece of prose, not the least of which is because it would not have been so effective that way. We also might understand his theology less if it had been simple, since that is *much more time-bound* than symbolism and imagery are. As an example, one might compare the contemporary understanding and usage of person and nature, which are conceptualized nowadays almost exclusively in psychological terms. This is quite different from the classical usage and understanding of these terms in philosophy and theology. Thus in any christological discussion much explanation is now required.

Revelation's "code" is not so undecipherable: there are certain universal and archetypal images that transcend cultures and ages. For example, red is easily understood as referring to bloodshed. Evil is often described in terms of darkness; good in terms of light. Yet the best approach to the symbolism is not to think of it as a code; there is not necessarily a one-to-one correspondence of x = y. Neither are the symbols allegories or predictions of the end of the world. The symbols are best approached like the notes in a musical score or the brush strokes of a painting: taken individually they do not mean much or can easily be misinterpreted. Taken as a whole, they convey a reality greater than the sum of its parts. Sometimes symbols have more than one meaning, even at the same time (another reason why we cannot approach this text as we might a modern allegory). Thus trying to create or determine a cipher, as it were, to Revelation is not the best way to approach the book. Rather, developing an appreciation for symbol, images, ancient rhetoric, and storytelling, as well as knowledge of the Old Testament, is a better way to "crack the code" used in the book.

19. The four horsemen bring their respective destruction to only one quarter of the earth. That tells us at least two things. First, these seals cannot be the end of the world, since 75 percent of it is left. Thus the interpretation that understands them to be a description of the general situation that humanity finds itself in is highly plausible. In other words, because of the Fall and original sin, humanity has been prone to war and violence (first and second horsemen), inhumanity and injustice (the third horseman is famine), and with sin comes death (fourth horseman). Second, the fact that the four horsemen come forth as a result of the Lamb's command subtly indicates that the havoc humanity wreaks on itself is within the scope of divine providence—however mysteriously—that is to say, there is a limit to the evil God will allow humanity (or will allow Satan; see Job) to perpetrate.

20. One of the hardest things to understand is John's view of time and history. One popular view is to interpret the whole of Revelation, especially the septets of the seals, trumpets, and bowls, as referring to the end of the world. However, this is too facile an approach and is, furthermore, also unsupported by the text itself. John does not offer a

blueprint for the history of the world or the Church and neither does he foretell the future of humanity. He does, however, like other major biblical prophets, prophesy God's word. Accordingly, his theology sometimes does concern the future or the end of the world.

Most interpreters understand the sixth seal to be a symbolic description of the end of the world. The imagery of the sixth seal is based on descriptions of the great and terrible day of the Lord as told by the Old Testament prophets. The answer to "who can stand?" in 6:17 is illustrated in chapter 7, which follows immediately. The whole cosmos is involved in the final distress—neither can the Church avoid it—but God protects people so long as they are faithful. There is an implied exhortation to remain faithful, or to become so. So, the answer to 6:17 is that repentant evildoers and the faithful can in fact stand. As in the prophet Joel, the threat of calamity is meant to bring or to encourage fidelity, and as in Joel, only a faithful people can escape the disaster. Once again, John uses symbols to convey the utter cosmic upheaval, and much of this symbolism is Old Testament imagery that John has adopted and modified. The thrust of the symbolism is to convey the end of the world by its complete and irreversible reversion to chaos. As with other symbolism in Revelation, that is not meant to be a literal description of things to come.

21. The seals are often seen as Old Testament type plagues justly unleashed and poured out on the wicked at the end-times. In this view, the understanding of God is that he is always arbitrarily angry, unfairly punishing humanity. However, that is not the depiction of God here. Rather, God is portrayed as a fair judge who is also merciful and just, righteous in his anger. The martyrs' cry in the fifth seal is not vindictiveness but a plea for justice. In the Bible, innocent blood cries out to be avenged (e.g., Gen 4:10). Such vengeance belongs only to God because he, unlike fallen humanity, can be counted on to be just and merciful (as he is to Cain in Gen 4). Reparation from sin and evil

must be done. The scene illustrates that God is just, rendering judgment according to what is true and right, and not overlooking sin and evil, which would be unjust. He is also patient with the guilty and the sinner (Rev 6:11); the martyrs have to wait for God's patience to be exercised as he mercifully awaits repentance by the wicked. The violence in these seals demonstrates the extent and ugliness of the evil and chaos unleashed by sin.

Section Six:
Revelation 7:1—8:2

22. In 7:1 the faithful are sealed against the harm to come on those who commit idolatry, that is, who refuse to give due homage to God (7:1–3). By virtue of Revelation's multivalency—as we have seen, for example, in its description of Christ as Son of Man, Lion, Root, and Lamb—the 144,000 servants of God (7:3–8) are the same group as the multitude in 7:9–17, namely, the elect (saints), who share in Christ's triumph. The redeemed people of God as a whole, which include the faithful of the Old Testament, are symbolically represented by the twelve tribes of Israel times twelve, times 1,000 (7:4–8). Having twelve tribes with 12,000 each indicates a vast people comprised of both the old and new Israel combined. The 144,000 are reached by means of 12,000 times twelve. Square numbers often symbolize perfection, as 144 does here: the people of God reach their perfection by fidelity to God, expressed here in terms of worshiping him alone. The multiple of 1,000 indicates the people of God in its vastness, and so the 144,000 are the same group as described by the multitude of 7:9. The huge crowd of 7:9–12, therefore, is the same group as the 144,000 in 7:1–8, only described in a universal way, namely, people from every race, nation, and tongue, not just the people of the Mosaic covenant. Typical of John's concern for universal salvation, this second part of the

vision of the elect indicates that the saved are not limited to the ethnic Israel of old. It also shows that the 144,000 people are not meant literally.

As with the twenty-four elders, this redeemed multitude is especially characterized by joy and victory: long white robes and palm branches are biblical symbols of victory. They are the elect who have won the heavenly reward for faithfully following the Lamb, before whom they now stand and serve along with the heavenly host of angels, elders, and the four "living creatures," in yet another heavenly liturgical scene. There is another sevenfold doxology in 7:12 (cf. 5:12).

This redeemed multitude is described as the faithful who bore the "witness of Jesus" and came through the great distress (7:14); they washed their robes and made them white in the blood of the Lamb. This striking image refers either to baptism itself or simply to the redemption Christ won by his sacrifice (1:5). The point here is that eternal life is gained only through the blood of the Lamb. The elect serve God in his heavenly temple, along with the heavenly assembly, in ceaseless service because they are a royal priesthood, a ceaseless service that continues the worship they faithfully gave him on earth (7:15). The elect are made up of the old and new Israel, which includes people from every race and tongue (21—22).

23. After the potentially disturbing scenes of the first six seals, the serene and joyful scenes of chapter 7 are a welcome relief. This twofold vision of the redeemed people of God is meant to convey a theology of hope. Although humanity suffers from the Fall and seems trapped in sin and overwhelmed by evil of its own making, God can and will save it. Moreover, although humanity must face divine judgment, there is also divine mercy. God does not desire the death and damnation of sinners, but that they live and are saved. This twofold vision of the elect from every people who enjoy salvation demonstrates the hope that God's people have in divine mercy and goodness. Those who

serve God faithfully will be preserved and ultimately saved. The rhetorical effect on the reader is to create drama, to highlight the culmination that this seal brings to the septet so as to motivate persevering under distress.

24. The content of the seventh seal has baffled interpreters, so much so that some suggest the silence is necessary for God to be able to hear the prayers offered in 8:3–5. There is undoubtedly a connection between the seventh seal and the succeeding seven trumpets; 8:2 makes that clear. The content of the seventh seal, however, is the silence in heaven described in its opening, just as the four horsemen are the content of their respective seals.

   This short period of silence is meant to suggest the respite that the elect enjoy, that is, the rest enjoyed in heaven. It is also meant to be a warning to the disobedient among the people of God, who will not enjoy rest from their worldly labors unless they repent. John has rendered in "seal style" the same theme that is the major idea in Hebrews 3 and 4. There the author explains why disobedient Israel did not enter into the promised land, into God's "rest." The silence in heaven of the seventh seal is the rest given to the obedient people of God after their ordeal in the desert. Once again John is using new-exodus imagery to express his theology. The rest of the promised land is a type of the rest of the saints. The promised land was the temporal place of rest for God's people of old; heaven is the new promised land, that eternal place of rest for the new people of God made up of every tribe and nation.

   Resting in the heavenly promised land echoes the sabbath rest in Genesis 1. The elect are brought into the heavenly rest because they are faithful in worshiping the God of the covenant (7:1–3). John is encouraging his fellow Christians to be faithful to the new covenant in the Lamb by worshiping God alone. The reward of entrance into the promised land awaits the faithful. Not to enter it is the just punishment of idolaters and covenant breakers (Ps 95).

Like the Book of Joshua in its listing of each of the twelve tribes only once they have entered into the promised land, so too, chapter 7 lists each of the twelve tribes who have entered into the new promised land, only once they have made it. With a new exodus comes a new promised land, which like the earthly one, is distributed among the twelve tribes.

Revelation 7:15–17 pictures the reward here in Old Testament terms reread in light of Christ. God will shelter them. Their eternal bliss reflects fulfillment of real needs in Israel's dry, hot climate: people must be sheltered from the intense sun and have abundant water to sustain life. These images are used in Isaiah 49:10 to describe God's saving and liberating power. In 7:17 it is the Lamb who will shepherd the people of God, an allusion to Psalm 2:8–9 (2:27 and 12:5) to indicate the blissful messianic reign in which life is full (abundant water) and happy (21:6; 22:1, 17). The sheltering and shepherding presence of God is a gift given eternally to the faithful who share in Christ's victory. The background to this pastoral image is Isaiah 49, where the prophet describes a return to the promised land of God's people after the exile. This return is a new exodus and a new creation: God gathers his people to himself anew in the land, where he shepherds them after restoring them to the promised land. This is a day of salvation, a time of favor (Isa 49:8). John envisions heaven as a new homeland, the true promised land in which God's faithful and obedient people, those who give witness to the word of God and Jesus Christ, will finally have a perpetual sabbath in which to rest and worship the Creator who saved them (the sabbath was made for humanity to do so).

There is silence also because God rests: after re-creating the world by the incarnation and redemption in the Lamb, there comes the consummation of the kingdom of God, the ultimate sabbath of the new creation. Each of the other seals may be understood likewise to have been a half hour in length, though not silent, and so the history of the world is symbolized by three-and-a-half-hours whose corruption comes to an end in this last half hour by the mercy of God. The cosmic battle is over. In presenting the seals as chronicling the Fall of humanity and all of creation, they can be likened to the seven days of Genesis 1. When God rests on the seventh day, he clearly neither speaks nor performs other acts of creation. The silence in heaven of the seventh seal suggests the same: no speech, no deeds, and no movement. After the silence, God stirs (see the next part of Revelation) to consummate his kingdom. After the Fall of humanity, the silence of Genesis 1 was likewise broken by God's stirring to prepare for and establish this kingdom in the incarnation. As suggested by the allusion to Zephaniah 2, the silence is in part because God is about to execute final judgment on his great and terrible day. John's rereading of this text in the light of Christ is that, after this execution of judgment, God will re-create a new heaven and a new earth.

Section Seven: Revelation 8:2—9:20

25. The angels who stand before God in 8:2 are a group of angels who sometimes appear in Revelation and who are also known as the "angels of the presence." In Jewish lore there are seven of them, and they include the archangels Michael, Gabriel, and Raphael, the only three mentioned by name in the Bible. Once again, we see that there are many different kinds and functions of angels in Revelation. A point to be made here is that these angels perpetually serve God and are given the trumpets by him ("were given to them" is a theological passive, that is, the unnamed agent is God), so that the trumpets, like the seals, come from the divine will. The angel with incense, which represents the prayers of the saints in 8:3–5, functions to bring before God the offering of prayer. The casting of the embers to earth is often understood as the answer to their

prayers. A theological theme here is that God hears the prayers of the just. This introduction is a reassurance before the blowing of the trumpets.

26. The mention of one-quarter and one-third devastation in the successive septets suggests a relationship between the two and yet also a distinction. Thus the technique of recapitulation is corroborated here. More specifically, the first four trumpets are an elaboration on the first four seals (horsemen), that is, a fuller description. If we read them against one another, we can see that the first four seals concern the effect of the Fall on humanity directly, and the first four trumpets concern the effect of the Fall on nature directly; together they portray the devastating effects of the Fall on all of creation.

27. The last three trumpets are called "woes," indicating that they are especially devastating. There is no equivalent in the seals. It seems that the trumpets are woeful for at least three reasons. First, they are directed at specific groups of human beings, which is something we did not see elsewhere (even the four horsemen wreak only general havoc). This makes them like the plagues against Egypt, not simply by kind but by aim; the plagues against Egypt were aimed at the Egyptians so they would liberate God's people and give glory to God. In this parallel, Revelation wants to convey that the new people of God are undergoing a similar exodus and that the new Egyptians are those who persecute the Church, specifically the pagans of Rome who insist on its worshiping the emperor and the idols.

Second, the woes are clearly demonic. The angel of the abyss and the scorpion-locusts that come from there have the destroyer (Abaddon-Apollyon) as their king. These are fallen angels who are permitted by God to give distress to humanity (stars often represent angels in apocalyptic literature; the one fallen from the sky is clearly a fallen angel). The bizarre horses of the sixth trumpet are also released by angels once divine permission is given. The creatures of both these trumpets are neither natural nor unnatural, but rather supernatural. They obviously are not good or in league with God. They are hybrid monsters, a pictorial way of saying they are demonic. They come from the abyss and have the king from the abyss as their leader. The abyss is the abode of Satan and the fallen angels.

Finally, we know that the five and sixth trumpets are aimed at unrepentant idolaters because of what is said in 9:4 and 9:20–21. The idolatry humanity commits is instigated and supported by Satan and his minions, the fallen angels. This is a typical reading of the Fall in Genesis 2 and 3, and is clearly John's perspective as seen in the letters to the churches (chap. 2 and 3). The seventh trumpet is also a woe, but that will be covered in later answers.

These trumpets, like the plagues against Egypt, are directed at the enemies of God, in Revelation, the inhabitants of the earth. This specific group has not been mentioned since 6:10. One might well query how a fuller picture of the woes highlights the mercy and patience of God. The inhabitants of the earth are warned three times (the woes in Rev 8:13; 9:12; 11:14), indicating that they are given repeated chances for repentance. The twice-mentioned refusal to repent after the first two woes (9:20–21) suggests that the trumpets' purpose is to bring the ungodly to repentance. Moreover, the inhabitants of the earth do not die at the fifth trumpet (9:6). This is intended to show the intensity of the distress of sinners and their increasing obstinacy (like the Egyptians before them) in response to God's mercy.

28. In 9:14 there is the divine command to release the four angels bound on the banks of the great river Euphrates. These angels unleash a bizarre cavalry, destroying with demonic plagues (e.g., sulfurous fire). The Euphrates is always known in the Bible as the "great river," which is of course the great river of Babylon. So to say "the great river Euphrates" is in fact redundant. John is intentionally directing the reader's attention to understanding this

trumpet as having exile imagery and not just an exodus motif. The Jews were exiled to Babylon where they endured oppression and rampant idolatry and where they had no temple.

The Church in John's day faces a similar cultural context, for they are strangers and persecuted for refusing to worship idols. Here John encourages his fellow Christians to be faithful to true worship by reminding them that God alone is worthy of all worship. Idolaters are chastised so they will be moved to repent.

The four angels are like the four winds of Zechariah 2. In that prophecy, there is a silence of God before he stirs forth from his dwelling to save his people, that is, to bring them back from exile. The new Babylon will be defeated so that the new Israel can return home from its exile by a new exodus at God's hand. Then God will dwell in their midst again and there will be no harm or ruin.

Section Eight:
Revelation 10:1—11:18

29. Revelation scholars are divided on this important point. Many interpret this scroll as identical to that given to the Lamb in chapter 5. In this interpretation the idea is that the seven sealed scrolls have now been opened (10:2), and, therefore, what has preceded this point in the book is preliminary; the revelation really starts with chapter 11. Others interpret this scroll as distinct from the others, largely because in Greek the word literally means "little scroll" (*biblaridion*), not "scroll" *(biblion)* as in chapter 5. In this interpretation the little scroll refers not to the plan of redemption in the Lamb as in the other scroll, but to the prophecy that John must give, specifically in chapter 11 (10:11). Accordingly, this prophecy spells out the role that God's people, the Church, play in this plan. Whichever interpretation is adopted, however, one must say that this

little scroll is somehow related to the scroll of chapter 5 and the work of the Lamb in redemption because it is the same angel in both 5:2 and 10:1; the diminutive *little* also indicates a probable relationship.

It seems best, then, to interpret the little scroll as related in content to the scroll of the Lamb, so that the ultimate triumph of the followers of the Lamb (the Church in its role in the salvific plan) is the specific content of this little scroll, rather than the whole plan of redemption or even the final consummation of the kingdom. That this is the case is seen by the commission given to John in 10:11; he must prophesy about the destiny of God's people and its enemies, which is part of the divine plan. God's people will be vindicated but only after a great ordeal—a prophecy hard to accept by God's people because they will have to endure great persecution in doing their part in the consummation of the kingdom (chap. 11).

30. The Two Witnesses have characteristics that remind us of various Old Testament figures. First, they are clearly prophets (11:3), who wear penitential garb (sackcloth). Second, they are described as olive trees and lamp stands "that stand before the Lord" (11:4), imagery taken from Zechariah 4 where the reference is to Joshua the high priest and Zerubbabel the prince. Third, they have characteristics of Elijah and Moses: in 1 Kings 18 and 2 Kings 1, Elijah calls down fire from heaven, and in 1 Kings 17 and 18, he prevents rain (Rev 11:5–6). Moses turns water into blood and commands plagues (Rev 11:6). An important element in identifying the Two Witnesses is that all the characteristics are given to *both* of the Witnesses, not just to one. So they cannot be Elijah and Moses, or Peter and Paul, or any other pair. In fact, it seems best not to identify them with any individuals, but rather to recognize that they represent the testimony given collectively by the repentant and faithful Church. We know this in part because the temple and altar are measured for preservation (11:1–3); the faithful people of God (not necessarily individuals) will be saved in

the upcoming ordeal. Later we will see John explain this in more depth (chap. 12—14).

The role of the Two Witnesses is to bear testimony to the Lamb and to the word of God. They do so, in great imitation of Christ, even to dying in a similar fashion. This is the main reason we can identify them as the Church; John sees the Church's role as carrying on the Lamb's redemptive work of salvation. It does so by witnessing to the Lamb in humility and truth (sackcloth). The world (peoples, nations, languages, and kings) needs the Church to do this so that it might also be moved to repent. The Two Witnesses are victorious in the end, vindicated, and are sharers in the resurrection. God has promised other victors the same in chapters 2 and 3.

31. The interlude of the seals serves to connect the first six seals to the seventh, and is an elaboration of them. The interlude of the trumpets functions similarly. The overall purpose of this interlude is the fulfillment of God's mysterious plan of salvation. Its fulfillment is imminent and is something his prophets have announced in the past and which John as a prophet announces in the present. In the past, specifically in the Old Testament, the role of God's people in the work of redemption was important. That is why John must prophesy again. The new Israel, like the old, must be a light to the nations. How the Church will do that is described in 11:1–13, for the Two Witnesses symbolize the Church.

One of the major themes in the trumpets is the need for the repentance of those who are not sealed by God; the first two woes are aimed at them to bring them to repentance. The prophecy of chapter 10 and that of the Two Witnesses of chapter 11 come together to show that part of the plan of God's redemption in the Lamb is that his followers would by their witness bring the unrepentant to repentance. Chastisements alone cannot do it. After some are said to repent (11:13), the prophetic activity is over and the seventh trumpet is blown. The kingdom of God has come into its final completion. Thus, the perfection of God's plan dawns, as announced in the interlude. The seventh trumpet is the third woe, which is told in 11:18. The time of judgment and damnation comes when the kingdom is fully consummated; it is not just salvation for the just but judgment on the wicked.

This interlude also looks forward to what comes after the trumpets. It introduces the story of chapters 12 to 14. Here we meet the Beast for the first time (11:7), and we learn of the great persecution of the Church (in the Two Witnesses) before the end of human history. What we learn then, from this interlude, is that God desires the Church to bear faithful witness so as to bring the nations to worship him. Their repentance is brought about not just by chastisements but also by humble testimony in *imitatio Christi*. The only repentance we actually see in Revelation is found as a result of the Two Witnesses' activity (11:13).

Active participation of the faithful in the Lamb's work of redemption will bring others to faith. Thus, for Revelation the Church is the new Israel, the new people of God, a light to the nations. It is the nations who are said to repent. They repent of their idolatry ("give glory to God" is a term for conversion from idolatry). This interlude is also part of the sharper focus of this septet. As in the seals, it is the same two groups in this interlude who make up the elect: the true Israel and the repentant nations. The openness to repentance, typical of the nations but not the inhabitants of the earth (who are never said to repent), is brought to the forefront. The nations are converted in part by the death of the Two Witnesses (they stare at them in astonishment; 11:9), while the inhabitants of the earth gloat— the latter have hardened hearts.

32. One of the best-known features of the book is its use of symbolic numbers. Forty-two months are $3^1/_2$ years or 1,260 days (calculated at 30 days a month, a lunar calendar). Typical of apocalyptic literature and the ancients in general, numbers were understood to hold objective val-

ues, some numbers being "good," others "bad," much like seven is "good luck" and thirteen is "bad luck" in our culture. Since seven is a perfect number, three-and-a-half represents imperfection. In Daniel, it is used to represent the persecution of Israel by a religiously intolerant pagan tyrant. John takes that number and uses it to speak of the persecution of the new Israel by a similarly intolerant pagan tyrant. John uses forty-two when speaking of the persecutors, but 1,260 when speaking of the persecuted. Revelation symbolically represents the period of great persecution against the Church with these numbers. The Two Witnesses are unburied for three-and-a-half-days (although three might have been expected, in connection with the resurrection of Christ) after the Beast has waged war against, conquered, and killed them. The struggle between the Church and its enemies will be told in more detail in chapters 12 to 14; here it is foreshadowed in part by the use of these symbolic numbers.

33. John is told by the angel to measure the temple and altar of God and those who worship there. This measure is an act of preservation, not destruction: God will preserve those who faithfully worship him (as in the sealing in 7:3–4). Idolaters will be destroyed; this is the meaning of not measuring the outer court. This temple is understood by many to be the Temple of Jerusalem, a symbol of the people of God. John lived through its destruction by the Romans in AD 70 and now uses the image of its preservation to indicate that those who worship God and the Lamb will not be condemned, as the old Israel was for refusing to worship the Lamb (and so it lost its temple). Jerusalem is the great city where the Lord was crucified and where the Temple stood. There will be a new, heavenly Jerusalem where the elect will dwell with God. In the meantime, the Church will be preserved, symbolized here as the temple and altar.

34. The seventh trumpet, like the seventh seal, seems a bit anticlimactic because, like the seventh seal, it simply announces

its content without description or elaboration. Like the seventh seal, the seventh trumpet will connect to another septet that follows. The elaboration of its content will come later in the book.

Section Nine: Revelation 11:19—12:18

35. Throughout the history of the interpretation of this text, this Woman has been variously identified. Many interpreters approach identifying her in terms of an "either/or" question: is she the Blessed Virgin Mary or is she not? To put it in these terms is to ask the wrong question. Rather, asking what the symbolism and narrative tell us about her identity is the key to discovering it.

The Woman is celestially clothed with the sun, stars, and moon. She is in the throes of giving birth. Her child is a son, a male child (literally, in the Greek), who is to rule (literally, shepherd) all the nations. This is a key point: this son can only be the Messiah. This child is then saved by God from the Dragon, who attempts to devour him at birth; the child is taken to God where he is enthroned. Most interpreters will understand that in these few passages we have the story of the incarnation and ascension of Christ told in abbreviated fashion. If the child is Christ, and there is no reason to say otherwise, then must not the Woman be the Blessed Virgin Mary? But there are other considerations. In 12:13–17 the Woman is pursued by the Dragon. She is given eagle wings and taken to the desert by God, where she is protected for the period of persecution. The Dragon is defeated again. He gives up on her and goes off to "make war on the rest of her children." Here is where interpreters often split: If the Woman gives birth to the Messiah, then she must be the Blessed Virgin Mary; yet, if she has other children in addition to Christ, how can she be the Blessed Virgin Mary? This is a question that a Catholic would raise.

If one takes the whole picture presented here of the Woman, instead of focusing narrowly on its individual pieces, and, if we understand that chapter 12 employs symbol and myth, then we can approach a solution. We have already seen that Revelation draws heavily upon the Old Testament, especially the prophets. Typical of the Old Testament and apocalyptic literature is to represent cities or peoples as women. Jerusalem, for example, is called "daughter Zion," "mother Zion," or "virgin daughter Israel," and so on. John employs this same symbolism here. Old Zion (Israel) gives birth to the Messiah, and then becomes the new Zion. It is mother Zion (Jerusalem) that gives birth to the Messiah, and it is Israel that is the rest of her offspring.

John is telling in a mythological fashion the story of the new Israel, the new people of God. The Zion of the new Israel is personified here as enjoying heavenly attributes: pursued by an evil serpent on earth, but protected by God. That is the situation of the new people of God in the present evil age, according to chapter 12. This new Zion, this new people of God, is comprised of all who "keep the commandments of God and hold the testimony of Jesus" (12:17), in other words, the Church. John is fleshing out the picture he presented in chapter 11, which introduced major characters. Also recall that in Revelation, Christ is simultaneously represented as a lamb, a lion, and a root, so that multifaceted symbolism for the people of God can be anticipated.

It makes sense that the Woman clothed with the sun is the Church (a people) because she has heavenly attributes and yet is enduring persecution on earth. After being told of the Church's persecution and the intimate connection between the work of the Lamb and the Church in chapter 11, we see it told in mythological fashion here. If the Woman is the Church, then she can also symbolize the Blessed Virgin Mary, insofar as the Blessed Virgin Mary typifies the Church (virgin, mother of all Christians, new Eve; see *Lumen Gentium*, VIII). Many commentators have seen this Woman as the new Eve also because she is called only "woman" (Gen 2:23), is obedient to God, is mother of all Christians (Rev 12:17), and defeats the serpent (Gen 3:15).

In sum, the Woman represents a people, namely, the new people of God, the Church. As the Church she is the new Eve who cooperates in the redemption of the Lamb, and is typified by the Blessed Virgin Mary. We have already seen that John employs multivalency. We will encounter this Woman again in Revelation. When we do, this identification of her here will be confirmed.

36. In contemporary American parlance, the word *myth* connotes a falsehood, an untruth, or a fiction, as, for example, in statements like these: "There's no such thing as unicorns; they're a myth," or "Global warming is a myth." But in the ancient world and the biblical milieu, myth is a story that conveys truth. The word *myth* in fact comes from the Greek word *mythos,* which simply means "story." Myths are a particular kind of story. They convey truth and the meaning of reality, especially religious truth and meaning, but in a way that is neither scientific nor historical. Yet neither are they necessarily a-scientific or a-historical; they simply do not have a scientific or historical view as part of the means for conveying their message. This is because the purpose of myth is not to relate history or science, but, rather, to relate truth and meaning in a story fashion. The meaning of deep realities that concern the human person, like love, cannot be explained by cold, rational data, and so myth has been an important tool for virtually every human culture, especially in the prescientific world. Some might argue that science has replaced myth in our culture.

Revelation uses myth here to tell the truth about the situation that the Church finds herself in and the religious meaning of that situation. Certainly John could have told this truth and meaning in other ways, like in a philosophical treatise, but it would not have been able to convey his theology with as strong an impact or with as lasting an impression. Stories remain with us, and we get caught up in their plots and resolutions. If John wanted to deliver his theology in a way that would visually and viscerally grip his audience, he succeeded by utilizing myth here. Recall that one of John's overall purposes is to move his audience to fidelity and steadfastness in the face of persecution.

One reason that the mythology of chapter 12 was powerful to John's contemporary audience is because they would immediately recognize and identify with the ancient myths. The cult of the emperor made use of the pagan myths to convey its religious ideas and to deify Rome. Another reason is that it is ingenious to cast the story of Christ in the terms of the familiar pagan mythologies, especially in a context in which there were pagan converts. The myth of Apollo in particular provides the pattern for this story: as he is about to be born, the serpent Python (the Dragon) attempts to devour him. Part of his escape is the use of water to foil the enemy. Apollo was one of the favorite gods of the Roman emperors, who would often depict themselves on coins as Apollo, the sun god. It did not take long for pagans who converted to Christianity to "baptize" this imagery and use it to depict Christ as the true Sun God (as in the art of the catacombs). Subtly and powerfully, then, John says once again that the real imperator is not Domitian but Christ; the Roman emperor is not divine, but Jesus Christ is.

Another very popular pagan idol was Diana, or Artemis, the twin sister of Apollo. She was the goddess of the hunt and was depicted with the moon. The temple to Artemis in Ephesus was one of the seven wonders of the ancient world, and Ephesus itself was the capital of the Roman province of Asia (and so first in the list of the seven letters). Artemis was the chief idol of the important imperial city Ephesus (see Acts 19, the riot of the silversmiths). Artemis would have easily been seen as the personification of the Roman Empire ruled by the sun god. Rome was also personified as a goddess in her own right (*Dea Roma*). The

Bible itself also provides mythological background to this chapter in the sea monster Leviathan and the land monster Behemoth. The former in particular provides a biblical precedent for a many-headed dragon (see Isa 27; Job 40—41; Ps 74:14; Bar 29:4).

What John has cleverly done is to retell the Church's story in the symbol and imagery of the imperial cult, which used the pagan mythologies. The true imperial home of Christians is not *Dea Roma*, but the Church, who is here depicted in terms reminiscent of Diana-Rome, only better. The true ruler of the universe (and all its empires and kings) is Christ, who is likewise depicted in terms reminiscent of Apollo, only better. The mythology provides a combined "replacement and one-upmanship" technique. Anyone in John's contemporary audience would immediately recognize this. The difficulty is that we modern Westerners find these myths inaccessible. We do not find myth in itself inaccessible, however, if the success of *Star Wars* and *The Lord of the Rings* is any gauge. In fact, we moderns are still gripped by the power of myth, and precisely because they do convey truth and meaning in ways that deeply compel us. If we realize that the myths of the Bible are true, that they are not fiction, and that there is more than one way to convey truth, with the scientific and historical only two of those ways, then we can begin to read chapter 12 with profit.

The incarnation of the Son, his birth of a virgin, his miracles and teaching, his resurrection and ascension, his eternal Godhead: probably all sounded very mythological to the ancient ear, pagan and Jew alike (consider Paul and the unknown god in Acts 17). The ancients were used to thinking about religion in mythological ways, and they knew that myths convey truth. They also knew, however, that the elements of the story of the incarnation were also factually and historically true.

What Revelation 12 does is put the true story of Jesus Christ in Roman mythological dress: a male child destined to rule the nations, pursued by a monster but protected by

God, then enthroned, and so on. This way of conveying the truth of Christianity would resonate with John's audience, comprised of converted pagans and Jews alike. Christ replaces the ancient myths, or rather fulfills them (sanctifying and perfecting them). The pagan myths can be likened to the Old Testament types in that they foreshadow Christ who fulfills them. John has taken the story of the incarnation and "Romanized it" in order to convey a principal point: the real story of a man-god is the incarnation of the Son of God, not an emperor who is deified as Apollo or Zeus.

From a purely biblical, mythological standpoint, the seals and trumpets emphasize that humanity is fallen and in need of redemption. The myth of the Fall in Genesis 2 to 3 is now "answered" by the myth in Revelation 12. With the use of myth in chapter 12, John has spoken universally, both to ancient pagans and Jews, and even to modern Westerners.

37. If one looks closely at 11:19—12:17, one sees that there is a main story that frames a minor one. In other words, in the middle of the story of the Woman in 11:19—12:6 and 12:13–17, there is a shorter story told in 12:7–12. This shorter story is about a war in heaven, in which the angel Michael defeats the angel Satan. The connection to the Woman's story is the figure of the Dragon, who attacks her and her child. The Dragon is identified here as Satan (12:9). This is no ordinary dragon: it has seven heads with diadems and ten horns, is red and large, and is an unnatural monster, clearly demonic. More will be said about the Dragon in the next section.

This short story is meant to illuminate the one that frames it. John has made a "literary sandwich," the "meat" of which is this story. In Revelation, there is the notion of a cosmic battle. This battle over humanity's soul is an old one, beginning long before the incarnation. The story has collapsed the telling of the fall of Satan into a mere six verses, but enough of the elements remain so that the reader gets the gist: Satan and his minions rebelled against

God and were defeated by Michael and his army. Michael is the patron of the old Israel (Daniel) as well as the new. Satan was so angry at being defeated and cast to the earth that he raged in fury with an insatiable desire to bring humanity to damnation. This is why he pursues the Woman and her offspring. He knows he must defeat her Child, and when he cannot, he pursues her other offspring. But Michael will protect those offspring; Revelation says the Church is protected, though individual Christians may suffer martyrdom.

Satan is identified here as the deceiver of the whole world and the accuser (*Satan* in Hebrew means "accuser"). The hymn of 12:10–12 proclaims that with the defeat of Satan, the kingdom of God and his Messiah can be perfected. This is an important point: evil must be vanquished before the kingdom can be fully consummated. Satan is particularly enraged because he knows that his days are numbered (12:12); it is only a matter of time now before he is completely vanquished. The language is clearly that of warfare: Michael wages war, and Satan is conquered by the blood of the Lamb. The earth and sea are warned that what Satan will do is woeful and that it is a result of his great wrath. Christians can likewise conquer him by the blood of the Lamb and their witness to him, especially in the ultimate witness that is martyrdom. This is exactly how the Two Witnesses conquer. The Woman's child is destined to rule all the nations; here the reign of the Messiah is proclaimed.

The essence of this story provides the theological lens through which to read the larger frame. In fact, these stories are mutually interpretive, both illustrating that salvation is twofold: salvation requires the total defeat of Satan as well as the incarnation-resurrection-ascension of the Messiah. The Woman and Michael are key in the salvation drama.

38. Once again we have symbolic numbers: 1,260 days (12:6), the length of the Woman's nourishment by God in the

wilderness, which is also described as "a time, and times, and half a time" in 12:14 (a direct borrowing from Dan 7:25; 12:7). Recall that the 1,260 days is the length of the period of testimony by the Two Witnesses (Rev 11:3), during which the "holy city would be trampled" for 42 months. These numbers are all equivalent ("times" = years). In Daniel the persecution of the Jews is for $3\frac{1}{2}$ years, the period of the desecration of the Temple in Jerusalem by Israel's pagan oppressors. John likens the persecution against the new people of God, the new Zion, to this one of old. In Daniel the persecutors are pagan idolaters who desecrate the Temple in Jerusalem by setting up a statue of the king in the guise of Zeus (the "desolating abomination").

In John's day, Domitian claimed to be a god and had his image on coins struck in the guise of Apollo. The persecution in Daniel and in Revelation is launched against God's people because they refuse to commit idolatry and instead worship only the living God rather than the head of state. The number 1,260 is significant: it is the sum of all the consecutive whole even numbers from one to seventy (so, 2 + 4 +...70 = 1,260). Moreover, seventy is seven times ten and therefore is often used to represent God's people (e.g., Jacob is said to have seventy sons). Seven is symbolic of perfection and ten of completeness. The number 1,260 is used only of God's people in this book. Here is another connection between the Two Witnesses and the Woman; in fact, this connection indicates that they are identical. Since the number three-and-a-half is half of seven, it is the perfect number to use in terms of persecution against God's elect. Forty-two is used of the persecutors; seven times six falls short of the perfection of the perfect number seven times itself, and so it represents the imperfection of God's enemies.

Section Ten:
Revelation 13:1–18

39. John identifies the Beast by the number 666, which stands for a person whose name can be spelled by numbers. As previously mentioned, the ancients understood that numbers have objective values. They loved to think of the universe in terms of numbers (like the 1,260 days or 42 months). They also used letters of the alphabet to count. So, for example, the year 2008 can be written in Roman numerals (i.e., in Latin letters) by MMVIII. Another example is that the Greek version of the Old Testament, known as the Septuagint (from the number seventy), is often written LXX for the seventy scholars who, according to legend, translated it. The same numerical spelling can be done in the Hebrew and Greek alphabets too.

Conversely, numbers can be used to spell. So, for example, the genealogy of Jesus in Matthew 1 uses the number *fourteen* three times to stress Jesus' Davidic ancestry. The number fourteen "spells" David in Hebrew by adding up the numerical equivalents of the letters used to spell the name. So, D = 4, V = 6, D = 4 add up to 14. This spelling was widely known and used in John's day. The now infamous 666 then would be easily "decoded" by John's audience. In an English-alphabet equivalent, in which a = 1, b = 2...j = 10, k = 20...s = 100, and so on, the name "John" would be designated by 128 (10 + 60 + 8 + 50 = 128).

When the numerical equivalents in Greek for the Hebrew form of the name "Caesar Nero" are calculated (i.e., added together), their sum is 666. In Latin they add up to 616, which is a variant in some biblical manuscripts (which corroborates this calculation). Nero (a Caesar) persecuted the Christians of Rome in a cruel and twisted fashion (e.g., using living Christians dowsed in oil and then set alight in order to illuminate the streets at night). He then becomes the personification in John's day for emperors who likewise persecuted the Church. Emperor Domitian, ruling about thirty years after Nero, is thus a new Nero. Nero's persecution of Christians was localized in Rome; Domitian's was carried on throughout the province of Asia and was government-sponsored.

The number 666 is especially meaningful to use for the archenemy of the Church of John's day. Six is imperfect because it is one short of seven. So 666 is triply imperfect, or superlatively so; that is to say, in Hebrew the superlative is made by repeating something three times (e.g., holy, holy, holy = holiest). So, the Beast is the most imperfect, thus the most evil. The name Jesus in Greek comes out to 888, and so he is the superlative of the new creation-resurrection since eight represents the new creation-resurrection. The number 666, as illustrated by Bauckham (*The Climax of Prophecy*, 393), is a doubly triangular number. There are in ancient geometry square, rectangular, and triangular numbers.

The familiar biblical example of a triangular number is the 153 fish caught in John 21. The number 153 is the triangular number of seventeen. Triangular numbers are found by adding consecutive whole numbers (1 + 2 + 3...17 = 153). The number 666 is the triangle of thirty-six, which is itself the triangle of six. Thus 666 is a *triply* triangular number. According to Bauckham, triply triangular numbers are very rare. Thus the use of one by John to designate the archenemy of the Church indicates he is particularly evil. (For more on this, see Bauckham's *The Climax of Prophecy*, chapter 11, "Nero and the Beast.")

40. The Beast, like the Dragon, has seven heads and ten horns, but it is described in reverse order (ten horns and seven heads) to show the connection and the distinction simultaneously. It has blasphemous names on its head and is a combination of a leopard, a bear, and a lion. It has one head that was mortally wounded but now healed, a direct parody of the Lamb that was slain but now lives. This also plays on the legend of Nero, who died in AD 68 by stab-

bing himself in the throat. The legend said he would return to life and rule again.

John and the Church of his day took this legend and used it to emphasize the wickedness of Domitian, who seemed to embody Nero; he was a Nero *redivivus*. Like Nero, Domitian also insisted on being worshiped as a god and put to death those who refused to give him such homage. He liked the title "our lord and our god" (cf. John 20:28). He had a whole institutional setup to insure worship of the emperor, the cult of *Dea Roma,* and the celebration of monthly feasts to pay him divine homage. Anyone who refused to worship or participate in the imperial cult was arrested and usually beheaded. Christians were considered bad citizens and atheists because they did not worship the emperor. Jews, of course, would likewise object to worshiping a man as God, but they were given legal protection from this law. Christians did not yet have this legal protection or right of religious liberty (and wouldn't until the fourth century).

The Beast—the first beast—is understood to be Domitian, put in place by Satan's (the Dragon's) power and authority. The second beast represents the official governmental bodies, offices, priests, and so on, that carried out the imperial cult (which animated the second beast), enforcing the worship. Thus did Domitian wage war (13:7) against the Church. The second beast is therefore aptly described like a ram that is a mouthpiece (a false prophet) for Satan. Its ram quality mimics Christ. We know that the number seven symbolizes perfection, and in the case of the Beast, he is perfectly monstrous. The seven heads mimic the Lamb—and Rome, of course, had seven hills. Horns typically symbolize power. The Beast then seems to be all-powerful, at least in an earthly realm. The second beast, who is a false prophet, performs signs. It does so to deceive people into worshiping the Beast rather than the Lamb. The stamped image of the Beast on the right hand or the forehead is the sign of allegiance of belonging to the Beast. It is a parody of the seal of the living God on the foreheads of the faithful. The forehead and right hand are visible to all so that ownership and allegiance are easily known and public.

41. In Revelation there is a "book of life" kept by the Lamb and God. It is a metaphor for eternal life, and indicates that all life comes from and is supported by God. God must sustain life or it dies; and it is only he who gives eternal life. There is more than one translation of 13:8; look at the variants in the New Revised Standard Version (or any translation with critical notes). John is not envisioning predestination, that is, that the inhabitants of the earth have been eternally damned before the world even came to be, although he is suggesting that the book of life has existed since then. One valid way to translate this without an emphasis on predestination is as the NRSV note has it: "...written in the book of life of the Lamb that was slaughtered from the foundation of the world." Neither does 13:9 suggest predestination, but rather a prophetic warning ("let anyone who has an ear listen") that the matter is urgent with no time for a change in one's destiny. The faithful, then, are exhorted to continue to be steadfast in fidelity to the word of God and the testimony of Jesus, if they want to remain in the book of life, that is, get to heaven.

Section Eleven:
Revelation 14:1—15:4

42. Mount Zion is the part of Jerusalem to which the Messiah is supposed to come when he at last establishes his reign (see e.g., Ps 2). It is the mount associated with the Temple. The Lamb, who is also the Lion from the tribe of Judah and the Root of David, is the Messiah. Recall that a major theme in Revelation is the final consummation of the kingdom of God. That is why the book's major images include God enthroned and the exalted Christ as imperator-king.

In the seventh trumpet we were told that "the kingdom of the world has become the kingdom of our Lord and of his Messiah" (Rev 11:15). The Messiah will reign over God's kingdom forever. However, evil and its kingdom must first give way; it must be utterly destroyed. This is the context for 14:1–5: the Lamb, who is the Messiah, together with his army, will defeat the tyrannous reign of evil in order to usher in fully the kingdom of God.

The Lamb has an army of 144,000. This is the same group of the elect, marked with the seal of the living God, from the twelve tribes, who had made their robes white in the blood of the Lamb (chap. 7). Here we have explicit language and imagery for war—and not simply war, but more precisely, biblical holy war. The Messianic Lamb has an army of the elect. They are completely faithful to him, "following him wherever he goes." They sing a new song, which happens only when God is doing something significant in carrying out his plan of salvation. Only those ransomed (or bought back) from the land (or earth) know this song: they conquer in war against the Beast by the blood of the Lamb (12:11).

In biblical holy war, a census of warriors was ordered by God, counting the number available to fight from each tribe. That is another meaning of the listing (numbering) of the twelve tribes in chapter 7, and why there is a numbering here. The Lamb's army is vast and ready. There were rules for biblical holy war: the warriors had to avoid sexual relations and to bathe ritually in preparation for war. When Israel received the Law at Sinai it had to do likewise (Exod 19—20). The army of the Lamb is pure, therefore, not having violated the regulations for holy war, but there is a mixed metaphor here. They are also "virgins...ransomed from humanity, first fruits for God and the Lamb." They are blameless, with no falsehood in their mouths. They not only follow the Lamb wherever he goes, they participate in his redemptive activity.

The Lamb is the sacrificial Passover Lamb that ransoms and saves by his sacrifice. The Passover Lamb must be without blemish (blameless) and a yearling male. The warriors are depicted as men (reasonably, since it is ancient Middle Eastern warfare) who are likewise without blemish, that is to say, they are ritually pure. The army of the Lamb, like him, is also without falsehood or blemish. The mention of first fruits prepares the way for what follows in chapter 14 in the imagery of harvesting. The difference between the Dragon and the Lamb is described in terms of truth and falsehood. The Dragon, who is the deceiver of the whole world, and those who worship the Beast are all liars steeped in falsehood. The Lamb is the Truth and there is no lie in his faithful followers' mouths. With this holy-war preparation scene, the language of conquering and victory in Revelation is fleshed out a bit more. In the Old Testament, Israelites who became idolaters were metaphorically said to have committed adultery or harlotry. To speak of the Lamb's army as virgins highlights their fidelity to him, morally, ritually, and cultishly.

43. In 14:6–13 three angels make pronouncements while flying in midheaven. The first one heralds the eternal Gospel to the inhabitants of the earth and to the nations, both distinct groups to whom the Two Witnesses give their testimony. They are called to worship God, not the Beast, because he is the Creator, the living and true God of all the universe. The same expression is used here of conversion ("fear God and give him glory"), found in 11:13, where we are told people converted as a result of the testimony of the Two Witnesses. This first angel's call for repentance in the face of God's imminent judgment is—like the first woe (fifth trumpet)—aimed specifically at those who are not sealed by the living God. It is a universal call to repentance.

The second angel proclaims that Babylon the great has fallen. We have not yet been introduced to Babylon, though we have seen new-exile imagery. Like the first angel's pronouncement, this too is a proclamation of judgment. Babylon is judged for perverting the nations. This is connected to the second woe (sixth trumpet) in the explicit reference to the great river, the Euphrates. In that woe, people in Babylon do not repent of their evil deeds, including fornication and idolatry.

The third angel announces the wrath and judgment of God on those who worship the Beast. This judgment is for the unrepentant, who deserve to drink the cup of God's wrath because they have refused him due worship. It is connected to the third woe (seventh trumpet) in that it elaborates on the advent of God's wrath and on the final judgment announced there (11:18).

The pronouncements of these three angels remind us, then, of the three woes, particularly of the urgent need for repentance of idolaters. Coming after the portrayal of the Beast and its demand for worship, this theme is thereby emphasized. There is also an emphasis on the urgent need for steadfast fidelity of those who are faithfully keeping the word of God and the testimony of Jesus. The promise of eternal happiness is given in 14:13 to those who persevere, a consoling contrast to 14:9–11. Notice that the warriors in the Lamb's army bear the Father's name on their foreheads (14:1), whereas those who worship the Beast have its mark (666) on theirs (14:11).

44. It is hard to say actually whether this is one bipartite scene or two separate harvests. John, however, by the use of his "then I saw" marker for new visions, makes it clear there is only one vision here, indicating that any sound interpretation must consider the two parts as somehow connected. Using the Old Testament background of harvests and vintages, Bauckham points out that 14:14–16 is really just a reaping that does not include the subsequent sorting of the harvest, that is, there is language only of reaping, of gathering in of the harvest, without any mention of winnowing or threshing.

In the New Testament, grain that is harvested but not sorted is used as a positive image for gathering into the kingdom (Bauckham's *The Theology of the Book of Revelation*, 94–98 and, e.g., Mark 4:29 and John 4:35–8). The next part of this vision, Revelation 14:17–20, is clearly vintage. The grapes are gathered and then trampled. This is an image of judgment. Oddly though, the grapes are gathered by a sickle, a violent image and literally a strange way to gather grapes that fits the language of wrath. The abundant wrath is similarly clear in how high the blood of the grape reaches. So here we have the outcome of the battle foreshadowed: the establishment of the kingdom and the judgment of idolaters will result when the Lord comes and the wrath of God and the Lamb are carried out.

45. Here John sees a vision of those who conquered the Beast. In their triumph, they sing to God a hymn of victory. This is the same group as the Lamb's army. They conquer not only the Beast but also its image and number, which would therefore include the emperor. Their victory will be total and complete. The new-exodus imagery here is hard to miss: the sea of glass mingled with fire is symbolic of the Red Sea. These victors have passed through it by the blood of the Lamb. They stand beside the sea, having reached the other side. Now on the other side, freed from the tyrant (the Beast; notice the emperor is set in the place of Pharaoh), they sing a victory song, as the old Israel did in Exodus 15 when it had reached the other side of the sea.

This new exodus has brought God's new people to the promised land of heaven, hence they hold the harps of God. The song they sing is of Moses and the Lamb because it is a new exodus in the blood of the true Passover Lamb. God's powerful signs and wonders—exodus language again—are praised. God's justice, truth, and holiness are glorified too, since that is how the victors have conquered: by having persevered in witnessing to these characteristics of God by their fidelity to him during persecution.

Section Twelve:
Revelation 15:5—16:21

46. The heavenly temple's tent of witness is opened by God in
    15:5, an indication of John's deepening vision. Recall that
    in 4:1 heaven is opened, and in 11:19 the temple of God in
    heaven is opened and the ark of the covenant is revealed.
    Now another aspect of the heavenly temple is revealed. In
    the exodus story, Moses is commanded by God to build a
    tent for the ark, a portable temple, as it were (since they will
    wander in the wilderness en route to the promised land for
    forty more years). Exodus 40 describes this temple, which
    is often simply called the dwelling, since this is where the
    Lord dwells among his people, enthroned on the ark. More
    often it is called the tent of witness (testimony). We are told
    that after Moses finished setting this up, the divine "cloud"
    covered the meeting tent and the "glory of the LORD filled"
    it. Moses could not then enter because the cloud had set-
    tled on the tent and the Lord's glory filled it. The cloud
    represents the presence of the Lord. During the forty years
    in the wilderness, Moses would consult the Lord in this tent
    (hence its names). There, when the cloud lifted, Moses
    would talk to the Lord "face to face."

    This background is necessary for understanding this par-
    ticular Revelation text. First, the new-exodus theme is now
    obvious. Second, if no one can enter the tent until the seven
    last plagues are over (15:8), that means no intercession is now
    possible, not even, it seems, by the new Moses (Moses was
    the supreme mediator for Israel during the exodus). These
    plagues are final, so the time for mediation is over. The note
    of urgency to repent in the previous portions is now clearer.
    These bowls are clearly instruments of judgment.

47. The seven angels holding the seven bowls that contain the
    final plagues are dressed in a way that may sound familiar.
    The Son of Man in 1:13 was dressed with a golden sash
    around his chest, an image of royalty. Bright white linen is

the way angels are often dressed, since white is the color of victory and purity. Linen was the fabric reserved for the priests' garments in the Old Testament. These angels serve the Son of Man, who is also King and Priest, and who reigns over a royal priesthood (a clear new-exodus motif). The army of Christ in 19:14 is similarly dressed because they share in Christ's kingly and priestly offices.

48. Every time these plagues are mentioned, the angels associated with them are too; they have high visibility in this septet. In 15:1 the great heavenly sign is the seven angels holding the plagues, not the plagues themselves, which gives emphasis to their provenance, that is, these plagues come from God. These angels are highlighted again in 15:5–6 as they emerge from the heavenly tent of witness. The four "living creatures" give them the golden bowls with the plagues of God's wrath. In 15:8 it is noticeable but not surprising, therefore, that the bowls are identified simply as the plagues of the seven angels. The point is that they come from God's heavenly throne. The angels who bear them and pour them out come from that throne in the tent of witness, which is presumably the ark.

   The bowls that hold God's wrathful plagues are golden. Golden bowls are often used in temple worship. Notice that twenty-four elders (5:8) offered golden bowls full of incense (which are identified as the prayers of the saints) in the heavenly worship scene in chapters 4 and 5. We are meant to understand that the bowls (or cups, chalices) are offerings to God, libations poured out one by one. The justice of God demands that his enemies drink the wine of his wrath, which we have just seen trodden out in 14:17–20. The thinking is that these libations both express and satisfy God's holy thirst for justice.

49. As with the seals and trumpets, the bowls have similarities to the plagues against Egypt in the exodus story. Though the first bowl is poured on the land (earth) only those with the mark of the Beast or who committed idolatry are struck

with the boils. This is similar to the sixth plague against Egypt. The second bowl is a plague on the sea, which turns to blood, similar to the first plague against Egypt. The third bowl is poured out on the fresh waters, which also turn to blood (again, first plague against Egypt). The fourth bowl affects the sun so that people are scorched. This has no Egyptian equivalent; however, the obstinacy that results is like that of Pharaoh. The fifth bowl plunges the throne of the Beast into darkness. This is similar to the Egyptian plagues in that it is aimed at the tyrant; also the ninth plague against Egypt is the plague of darkness on the Egyptians alone (in addition to boils again). They do not repent either. The sixth bowl has a similarity to the frogs in the second Egyptian plague. The seventh bowl contains hail, like the seventh plague against the Egyptians. John has modeled these plagues after those against Egypt in the exodus story in order to suggest a new-exodus theme, but they are not exact mirror images.

According to Numbers, the golden libation bowls were kept on the table of the presence in the tent of witness (Num 4:7) and were used in atonement of sin by pouring out the blood of the holocaust at the designated altar in the sanctuary (e.g., Lev 4:7; Num 4:8, 28:7; Sir 50:15). The angels who pour out the bowls in Revelation are offering sacrifice to the Lord in accordance with biblical practice. These plagues are part of worship duly offered to the Creator of the world and Lord of history.

50. The sixth bowl is poured out on the Euphrates, the great river of Babylon. We saw a reference to this river in the sixth trumpet. These references sound a new-exile note. This bowl is clearly aimed at the demonic. The satanic triad is targeted here (the second beast is called the false prophet), each having an unclean spirit like a frog. The new-exile imagery underscores the reality of the Church, which is persecuted by pagan idolaters in a strange land.

The seventh bowl mentions the divine judgment on the great city of Babylon. It splits into three parts as the result

178

of an unprecedented divinely instigated earthquake. God thereby renders punishment against hardened idolaters and those who persecute his faithful people.

51. The battle described in the sixth bowl occurs at "the place that in Hebrew is called Harmagedon" (Armageddon), which literally means "Mount Megiddo." Megiddo was a real biblical place, an important strategic site in the north of Israel (and even now is an impressive archaeological site). Significant and decisive historical battles were fought there, and because of that, Armageddon it is used to symbolize the place of the final defeat of evil by the forces of good. Because of this bowl, in contemporary, popular American thought, Armageddon has come to refer to the final battle or conflagration associated with the end of the world.

52. The pattern of the bowls is very similar to that of the trumpets. In the sixth bowl the way is made for the kings of the east to come by drying up the Euphrates. The froglike demonic spirits coming forth from the satanic triad use deception to gather all the kings of the whole world, to "assemble them for battle on the great day of God the Almighty" at Armageddon. This great day of God, a terrible period of divine wrath, was also mentioned in the sixth seal (6:17). With the seventh bowl, "It is done!"—and so it appears to be: the great earthquake, the splitting of the great city, and the cosmic upheaval are all of the same kind described in the sixth seal.

But what, precisely, is finished? At the very least, one has to say that, given the context of the bowls and the progression in the narrative from 11:19 on, what is accomplished is the divine judgment on Babylon. This judgment is told in familiar Old Testament terms and is located at Armageddon to underscore its definitiveness. Because the language of the great day of the Lord, an Old Testament way of speaking of the final judgment on all humanity, is used here, and because there is the final battle in the defeat of evil, it is reasonable to say there is a double meaning here, that is, John intends this specific imagery to apply to both his contemporary situation and to the ultimate consummation of human history. Evil must at last be destroyed before the kingdom of God is fully established.

53. There have been explicit references to Babylon and use of the language of new exile throughout Revelation. There have also been implicit references to the Roman Empire and various imperial realities. The First Letter of Peter speaks of Rome as Babylon while also mentioning Mark the evangelist, whose Gospel is addressed to Christians in Rome suffering under Nero's persecution (see 1 Pet 5:13). Rome was like a new Babylon in its corruption, idolatry, and persecution of God's people. Babylon is fittingly used in Revelation, therefore, to symbolize Rome. Rome prided itself on its greatness, and so rather tongue-in-cheek, John always says Babylon the Great.

Section Thirteen:
Revelation 17:1—19:10

54. In the Old Testament, whenever Israel committed idolatry, it was often spoken of, by the prophets especially, as adultery, harlotry, or fornication. One reason for this, is that the Lord was considered the spouse of Israel, so infidelity to him was naturally presented in this way. Another reason is that the pagan cults consisted of so much sexual license and religious prostitution (both genders) that harlotry is an apt metaphor. The Canaanite fertility cults sorely tempted Israel (see, e.g., Judg 1—2). Israel was frequently guilty of harlotry, metaphorically speaking, with the baals and the ashteroth.

It fits John's perspective and portrayal of the world in which he lived to symbolize Rome in this fashion: Rome was corrupt and its power and luxury seductive. Its imperial cult was likewise attractive, not the least of which was because it was the norm. The kings who cooperated with Rome were the pagan rulers and peoples who willingly became part of the empire and who took part in the *Pax Romana* to benefit from it (thereby prostituting themselves in other ways). The luxury and the corrupt morals of Roman nobility and rulers were notorious. The kings were drunk with her wine, for they had been seduced by her.

The Harlot in 17:3–7 is described as sitting on a scarlet beast full of blasphemous names. The beast is easily identifiable, with its ten horns and seven heads and, as the first beast (see 13:1–8). Its blasphemous names are those divine titles falsely assumed by the Roman emperors. The Harlot sits astride the Beast dressed in the colors of royalty and lavishly adorned. She holds a golden cup (libation bowl) filled with abominations and impurities. The cup looks wonderful to drink from and the woman desirable to know, but both are unclean and putrid. The desecration of the Jerusalem Temple by Antiochus IV (by erecting a statue of himself as Zeus on the altar; see Dan 7—12 and 2 Macc 6) was called by Daniel the "abomination of desolation" (8:13). The Harlot has a symbolic name on her forehead that identifies her as Babylon the great, mother of harlots and earth's abominations. Thus we know that the great Harlot is Rome and the scarlet Beast is the Beast of Revelation 13, the persecutor of Christians, Emperor Domitian *(Nero redivivus)*. This is confirmed by 17:6: the Roman empire had drunk the blood of Christians in martyring them. Many commentators suggest the Harlot astride the Beast is modeled here after the goddess Rome *(Dea Roma)*. This would make another nice parallel to the Woman of chapter 12; two cities-peoples personified as women, who are also depicted mythically. In 17:15–18 the Harlot's destruction is described in a gruesome fashion, foreshadowing what comes later. As Rome rules over many peoples, so does she sit on "many waters," and is the great city that rules over many kings and peoples (17:18).

55. From Revelation 17:6 and onward, the angel explains to John the mystery of the great Harlot and of the Beast on which she sits. The key factor in understanding the mystery is 17:8–9, which describes the Beast as "it was and is not and is to come," and having seven heads that are both seven mountains (hills) *and* kings. This description clearly mimics that of God and the Lamb: who is, who was, and who is to come, and who was slain but now lives. The seven hills are the seven hills of Rome, as well as the full count (symbolically) of its emperors. The real difficulty is how to understand that the Beast is an eighth king that is one of the seven; this fact must be combined with the detail that the Beast is a king that existed once and then did not, and now exists again. The best solution to this riddle is that this king is one of the seven, but also an eighth, and that he will remain only a little while—a play on Nero, who died of a self-inflicted stab to the throat, but who, according to legend, would return. The legend casts Domitian as Nero *redivivus.* There are various ways to count the Roman emperors of the first century, but this seems to fit best with the other data in Revelation (like the 666 = Nero). The symbolism of the heads as hills and kings has more than one meaning, typical of Revelation's multi-valency.

   That the scarlet Beast is Rome personified in Domitian-Nero is clear also from other data in chapter 17: the inhabitants of the earth are amazed at it (see chap. 13), it comes up from the abyss, and it goes to destruction. The ten horns are ten kings who allow Rome to rule in order to benefit from her. This is a foreshadowing of their demise (they rule for one hour, 17:12, and will fall in one hour, 18:10).

56. In the dirge over Babylon in chapter 18, there are three groups who mourn her: the kings of the earth (18:9–10), the merchants of the earth (18:11–17) and the shippers (18:17b–19). In short, the mourners are all those on land and sea who benefited from trading. The third group

really is a subset of the second (see 18:3, where these are the only groups). The kings are punished because they "committed fornication and lived in luxury with" the Harlot, and the others are punished because they "have grown rich from the power of her luxury." In both cases, the condemnation comes from cooperating with and benefiting from evil. These groups do not mourn Babylon-Rome for its own sake, but for their own financial ruin. They lament the loss of luxury and sensual pleasures, keeping their distance lest they too burn.

Rome is severely criticized here for its wealth and luxury and the wanton lifestyle that goes with it. The cargoes of the merchants make a detailed account of just how wide and varied the trade of the empire was in John's day. However, the greatness of Rome's wealth and power was built on slavery, trafficking in human lives (18:13), and on crushing the poor. The Roman system could not have been supported except with this kind of labor. This is one reason why, in 13:17, worship of the Beast is described so explicitly in terms of buying and selling. It is also one reason why St. Paul so readily uses terms like redemption and ransoming from slavery to describe what Christ has done for humanity. It is not money in itself John objects to, but the disordered sensual pleasures that it supports and the ruin of human lives it causes. These groups have put their trust in riches, rather than in the Lord God, committing idolatry more familiar in our own neopagan American culture today. John thereby subtly makes the point that worship also has very much to do with how one lives.

57. The way John describes the destruction of evil Babylon-Rome is marvelous. He never really describes the actual destruction, only its result, like the smoke going up from her burning (18:9), or as no longer inhabitable (18:2). It takes only a single hour, symbolic of a brief period, to destroy her because God's power is so mighty. Neither did it take long to destroy Pharaoh or Sodom and Gomorrah.... God's justice is swift and sure.

It likewise takes only a single hour because evil cannot last; its power is limited, and its days are numbered (12:10–12). Because evil is destructive, it eventually will destroy itself. John conveys the idea that Rome is not so great and mighty after all, because, like Babylon of old, when God comes at last to execute judgment, there is no escape and no more delay. Her plagues come in a single day, even in one hour, for the Lord God who judges her is almighty and she is nothing but putrid filth (18:8).

58. The kings and the Beast will make Babylon the Harlot "desolate and naked; they will devour her flesh and burn her up with fire" (17:16). This gruesome feast is "fleshed out," as it were, in 19:17–21. This feast of evil has its counterpart in the wedding feast of the Lamb, the feast of good. Heaven, of course, is often depicted in the New Testament as a wedding feast; likewise, the final consummation of the kingdom of God is so described here. The Lamb, who is the Messianic King, not only ascends his throne after the defeat of evil but he also takes a bride at the same time. This idea is typical of messianic texts. What we now expect to see more fully described, then, is his bride. Interestingly, so far we have seen a mother (chap. 12), a harlot (chap. 17—18), and now a pure bride. The Lamb's wedding feast heralds the final consummation of the kingdom of God, which is why those who are invited are blessed indeed (19:9).

59. In this passage, and also in 22:8–9, John responds to the truth of the revelation entrusted to him by paying homage to the angel of the presence who shows it to him. He does so not because he is an idolater, but in order to give due reverence to God, whom the angel represents, for revealing these mysteries. The angel explains that he (the angel), John, and Christians are all equal before God, that is, they are all creatures who owe God due worship. And so the angel calls for worship of God, *not as a correction,* but as an indicator as to how to interpret the scene aright. John is a

model of proper worship because he renders due homage to God, represented by the angel. The angel's apparent correction is meant to underscore the need for all Christians to do likewise.

Section Fourteen: Revelation 19:11—20:15

60. There are some religious sects that interpret the entire book as purely eschatological. They understand the whole of Revelation to be about the *eschaton*, in a coded prophecy that is applied to the current state and history of the world. Unfortunately, this truncated vision has saturated the popular view of the book.

On the other hand, one must really say that the entire book is eschatological. If eschatology refers to the hope that Christians have for the kingdom of God, then this interpretation is dead-on. That is the overall scope of the book because that is the overall scope of Christian hope. If with the incarnation, the kingdom of God is now among us (Mark 1:15 etc.), then for this reason, too, Revelation is about the end for all humanity since the incarnation of the Son of God lives in the *eschaton:* with the incarnation, the *eschaton* has broken into human history. This is certainly John's perspective: in chapter 12, the newly born Messiah is caught up to God's throne, and with the incarnation-death-resurrection-ascension, Satan's defeat has begun. For John, the kingdom has dawned in Christ, but its fullness will not be realized until his Second Advent. Typical of Johannine theology, Revelation has both eschatological views: that the end has arrived in Christ and simultaneously that it has yet to be fulfilled. For most of the book the story focuses on how, in the present evil age, the victory already belongs to the Lamb. Only in these final chapters is the focus on the last battle. Only in this last section are the specific four last things described (e.g., the *Parousia* and the last judgment).

Practically speaking, this means that not every vision or detail tells us directly about the end-days. John is writing to encourage his contemporaries and every generation of Christians to follow the Lamb. He never says, for example, *when* the end will come, except soon—a very relative term if to God a thousand years are as a day and a day as a thousand years (2 Pet 3:8). So reading the details as an encoded message in which the current age is the last one is problematic at best.

John's apocalyptic prophecy is not foretelling some divine blueprint for the future. It is, however, about the future in that it gives a picture of the ultimate defeat of evil and the consummation of good as part of the divine plan of salvation. John stirs up hope in Christian readers of every age so that they can see their own battle against evil in its proper context: the Church will prevail and the kingdom will come to its perfection because the Lamb has already won the war against the Ancient Serpent. As a biblical prophet John is speaking to the people of God about the meaning of the *present*. As a biblical prophecy, his word has a meaning that reaches into every generation since scripture is universal and timeless. Many of the details are time-bound (like 666) because the human authors of scripture *write* as authentic human authors (see *Dei Verbum* III), but their meaning is for all times and peoples. The bottom line is that the end-times have been ushered in by the incarnation, which changes everything—the cosmos, humanity's situation, and creation's destiny. For John, all Christians, individually and as a people, are called to live as if Christ were coming soon to judge and to save.

61. The careful reader will recognize that many of the details used to describe the heavenly Rider-Warrior are used of Christ elsewhere in Revelation. In particular, the vision of the exalted Christ in chapter 1 is echoed here in the mention of the sword that comes out of his mouth and in his

eyes that blaze like fire. He has an army like that of the Lamb in chapter 14, and he treads the winepress of God Almighty, also in chapter 14. Other elements of the depiction here tell us even more: he is the Word of God, the divine Logos coming from heaven, who reveals the Father and redeems humanity. He is a warrior-king: justice is his standard in waging war, that is, rendering judgment on the wicked and giving salvation to the faithful; he has many crowns. This is the messianic warrior-king of Revelation (12:5) who will defeat the Dragon and his armies.

He does so not with a literal sword but with his blood, shed on the cross, the sure means of victory for him and thus for the faithful. His unassailable word of judgment—definitive and commanding as a two-edged sword—is also an instrument by which he conquers. Christ is described in this packed picture as a messianic warrior-king to highlight John's idea that all the cosmos is locked in combat. Christ, who is King of Kings and Lord of Lords, will win the last battle and be victorious over Satan. This final battle is the beginning of the end. Christ is the true emperor, not Domitian. He is depicted here as the conquering hero in battle, much as a statue might depict the Roman emperor doing so. This depiction is meant to rouse the Lamb's troops, as it were, that is, to move the reader to be steadfast in the ongoing fight against evil, for we know to whom the victory goes.

62. In 19:20 there is a lake of fire that burns with sulfur. In the final battle, the Beast and the false prophet are not killed and left as carrion, but rather hurled into this sulfurous lake. John describes it in 20:10 as the place where Satan (Dragon) is also thrown. There the evil triad "will be tormented day and night forever and ever." In 20:14 we see that the last enemy, death itself (and the netherworld, the realm of the dead, also known as Hades or Sheol), is also destroyed by being hurled there too. This lake is called the second death. It is also the place where the damned are cast (20:15). It is now perhaps easy to identify this lake as hell,

the place of eternal torment of the damned. The image of hell as a place of fire is not new in Revelation.

63. The interpretation of the millennium in chapter 20 is probably the most complex exegetical task of this book. The interpretation of this one element has had many and various influences on doctrinal development throughout the history of Christianity. (For the various kinds of millenarian positions, the reader is advised to consult works like those of Olson, Corsini, Koester, or Wainwright. See the bibliography.) In the most basic terms, there are essentially two positions of interpretation: that the thousand years are to be understood literally or symbolically, which, of course, is the same basic positions of interpretation for the rest of Revelation, and that is the point really. If the symbolism, especially the numbers, in the rest of the book are not to be taken literally (e.g., 144,000 or 1,260), then neither is this number.

One thousand symbolizes a long period of time that is complete; it is an era or age. In ancient Jewish and apocalyptic thinking, it was common to represent the history of the world in seven successive ages of one thousand years each, a "cosmic week" of eras. That seventh age was often associated with the messianic era, an age of a blissful reign of peace and justice on the earth under the Anointed One (Corsini, 371). Sometimes there was an eighth millennium that represented eternity. The basic idea is that if the world were created in seven days, its history would be seven days of a thousand years each. The seventh day would be the sabbath rest, that is, the reign of the Messiah. This is undoubtedly part of the background to the Revelation of John: the age of the Messiah will come at last (see 11:17). But is the messianic reign earthly or heavenly, temporal or eternal?

What also must be considered in interpreting this millennium, however, is that it refers not just to the reign of the Messiah (20:4, 6) but also the period of the binding of Satan (20:2, 7). Satan is bound until the thousand years are over so that he does not lead the nations astray (20:3) dur-

Answers

ing that period. After this Satan must be released (divine necessity) for a short time, during which he will deceive the nations and muster his troops for the final battle, in which he is defeated.

Intertwined with all of this is the scene of judgment thrones of those beheaded for their witness to Jesus (20:4). They are raised up and share Christ's reign for a millennium, referred to as a first resurrection. Their sharing in his reign is emphasized, since it is mentioned twice (20:4, 6). Nowhere in Revelation is it said that this messianic reign is on the earth (that is read into this text here from 5:10). These two millennia are really only a single one, occurring simultaneously, but used as two to make a contrast: the establishment of the reign of the Messiah means the end of reign of the Dragon. The realm of Satan and his hold on the world is now demolished. This realm gives way completely to the Messiah. But this world also is at an end and will give way to the kingdom of heaven, where the messianic reign will take place. The contrast between the two millennia is subtle but significant. Satan's reign of a thousand years is limited in scope and power because he is bound, and in duration because it ends with his decisive defeat and eternal damnation (20:8–10). The Messiah's reign of a thousand years, however, is the age that will never end. It is the age of the new creation that his Second Advent ushers in. Those who have been faithful in witnessing to him will share his victory (as promised in the letters) by reigning with him. Satan's reign is earthly and temporal, but the Messiah's is heavenly and eternal.

The encouragement to John's fellow suffering Christians to endure faithfully is clear here: the just will be vindicated (represented by passing judgment in 20:4) over those who tried to make them commit idolatry (chap. 11). John wants to emphasize the reward of the blood martyrs. Because they have faithfully borne witness they will enjoy their reward, which is to reign with Christ eternally. Daniel 7 is certainly in the background of chapter 20, in which the kingdom is transferred from the Beast to the people of

God, who had been persecuted by him. The Beast is judged and condemned and the people of God are rewarded with life in the messianic kingdom.

Bauckham's interpretation of these thousand-year reigns in chapter 20 is most enlightening and helpful (*The Theology of the Book of Revelation*, 104–8). His main idea is that the key to understanding these texts on the millennia is *how they function*. The main point of the two contrasting millennia is to show the triumph of the faithful witnesses. The battle described throughout Revelation is that between the Dragon and the Woman, the Beast and the Two Witnesses (offspring of the Woman). The suffering and persecuted Church must be shown to be victorious, in accord with its share in the redemptive work of Christ and the victory of the Rider-Warrior. The exalted risen Christ is the only authentic universal emperor and conquering hero. Those who refuse to worship the Beast are at last rewarded. In this world, ruled by the Dragon, it appears as though the Beast wins, but ultimately it is those who are faithful to Christ who do. Thus the millennia show the meaning of this victory rather than a literal description of it. This conveyance of meaning, of course, is characteristic of Revelation and its use of symbolism. That the unmartyred faithful are raised after a thousand years then is no longer a problem— because it is not chronological but rather symbolic and spiritual in meaning.

64. The Rapture is used by some Christian groups and fundamentalist sects to refer to the "seizing or catching up" of Christians into the air to meet Christ when he comes in his Second Advent. It is a strictly literal reading of 1 Thessalonians 4:16–17. Non-Christians will, accordingly, be left behind (one interpretation of Luke 17:34–35). Some people who hold to this doctrine also believe it is intimately connected with a millennial reign of the saints (Christians) with Christ on earth at the close of human history. This view includes the rise of an antichrist figure who will deceive people into following him, and a seven-year

period of great tribulation from which Christians are spared because they have been "raptured."

This is oversimplifying it, but such is the general gist. Its permutations vary group by group. The most curious thing is that Revelation has no language or imagery of such a rapture. Neither does Revelation use the word *antichrist* (but see 1 John 1:18). There is certainly a tribulation in Revelation, but it is experienced by Christians. Revelation is quite clear on this point: the faithful suffer until Christ's Second Advent.

The term *Parousia* (Greek for "presence" or "arrival," usually referring to the visitation by a king) refers to the Second Advent of Christ in glory at the end of human history. Catholics, Orthodox, and mainstream Christian churches believe in this Second Advent (see, e.g., the Apostles' and the Nicene Creeds). They also believe Christ will be manifested in glory in his *Parousia* and that the events of the *eschaton* are tied to it. Once he comes again in open, unmistakable glory (not in secret), he will judge humanity (the last judgment) after the general resurrection. Only then will he consummate his kingdom. There will be a period of tribulation before the end, but this period is not specified, and no one will be spared. For Catholics, the Antichrist refers generally to people or institutions that oppose Christ, which will increase in the end-times when the Church will undergo a great trial and there will be a supreme religious deception with a false messianism that glorifies man not God (*CCC* 675–76).

Catholics believe that Christ is present even now in the Church and that he now reigns supreme over the universe. His Spirit enlivens and strengthens the Church in every age, including the *eschaton*. There is no need, therefore, for an interregnum of the saints on earth with Christ in literal, earthly terms. One of John's major points in Revelation is that there is no need for the Church to fear trial or persecution, or for a Christian to seek to be spared from them; God has and will continue to provide for the faithful, including the grace of patient endurance.

On these exegetical questions it is clear that how one reads the biblical text really matters. Whether one reads it literally or symbolically, the effect is doctrinal. But the doctrinal differences stem in part from the approach to the text. For an excellent discussion on the question of the Rapture and other matters, both in their literal and nonliteral interpretations, see Olson's *Will Catholics be Left Behind?*

65. The last-judgment scene in chapter 20 is reminiscent of Daniel 7. The Ancient One is seated in his kingly, heavenly court, and the final judgment, the great day of the Lord takes place. The books are opened, from which God renders judgment. The books are symbols illustrating that God's justice is fair, not arbitrary. The accounts are kept of every person's deeds, and judgment is made on that basis, nothing else. The deeds one has done on earth, in the body, are the criteria for judgment. The general resurrection must take place first. The biblical and Christian anthropology is that the human person is a whole, unified being with body and soul, therefore resurrection can only refer to the *whole person* (e.g., 1 Cor 15). So the bodies of the dead are raised and reunited with their respective souls. Whole persons are then judged, and likewise whole persons are then welcomed to enjoy resurrected life, or condemned to eternal damnation.

The last judgment, one of the last things, is associated with the Second Advent of Christ, which marks the end of human history. Even creation (Rev 20:1) does not desire to stand before the great Judge because it has shared in the sinfulness of humanity as a result of the Fall. With the general resurrection and the end of human history, there is no need for death or the realm of the dead (Hades or Sheol); God puts his last enemy to everlasting destruction.

Section Fifteen:
Revelation 21:1—22:5

66. Recall that in the salvation scene of 19:1–8 the announcement is made of the wedding feast of the Lamb, which foreshadows 21:1–8. Recall too that the ascension to the throne
for the Messiah is also celebrated as his wedding day. In
19:7–8 the Bride is ready: God has given her finest white
linen as her garment, that is, she has been dressed in the virtuous deeds of the saints. In 21:2, the new Jerusalem is the
pure Bride of the Lamb, prepared and adorned to meet her
Groom. This Bride, the spouse of the Lamb, is put in direct
contrast to Babylon the Harlot (21:9).

   This new Jerusalem described as the Bride is none other
than the people of God, the Church. But she is the people
of God transformed, that is, the Church Triumphant. The
Messiah, Christ the Lamb, takes her to himself forever in
his kingdom in an eternal union.

   As mentioned previously, the Old Testament covenantal
union between God and Israel was often spoken of
metaphorically in terms of a marriage bond. Revelation
does the same, and so the image of the people of God (the
Church) as the Lamb's Bride conveys intimacy between
God and his people. Revelation 21:3–4 describes the eternal intimacy and blessed joy of God's people in the new
creation, the kingdom of God, and the Lamb.

67. The Bride of the Lamb is explicitly identified as the heavenly Jerusalem in 21:9. She is clearly also the saved people
of God, bound in an eternal covenantal marriage-bond to
the Lamb. The heavenly Jerusalem has the twelve tribes of
Israel and the twelve apostles as its gates and foundation
(21:12–14). This symbolism of the old and new people of
God as constitutive of the heavenly Jerusalem indicates
that the faithful of both the old and new covenants will
enter the beloved city. The Woman clothed with the sun is
also to be identified as the people of God and the Church.

Even on earth the Church reflected the celestial reality of God; now in heaven she does so even more purely and brilliantly.

John does not, however, seem to envision the Church on earth and the kingdom of God in the heavenly Jerusalem as identical: the faithful Church on earth will be transformed and become part of the kingdom of God in heaven, incorporating the faithful old people of God and the converted members of the nations (21:24). The earthly Church does not already consist of these groups. This is consistent with John's call to repentance from his fellow Christians; only faithful Christians will enjoy the wedding feast of the Lamb, which is another way of saying that the Bride will be adorned with the virtuous deeds of the saints.

68. The heavenly Jerusalem is portrayed as a place of no evil, pain, suffering, unhappiness, corruption, or death. It is clearly paradise, a place of eternal bliss. The imagery of 21:4 is paternal: God himself comforting and healing his beloved people (Isa 25:8; 35:10). When God finally and completely destroys evil, its consequences and effects also disappear.

In the heavenly Jerusalem, God will shepherd his people. He will give them life-giving water, an image of eternal life (Isa 55:1). Both this image and the paternal one are intended to convey the depth of compassion, care, and love of both God the Father and the Lamb as Shepherd for the people covenanted to him forever.

69. By setting 17:1 and 21:9 in direct parallel, John forces the reader to compare the two women-cities. In both cases the women-cities are shown to John by one of the angels of the seven bowls, an invitation to come and see. Beginning with 17:1, there is the Babylon Appendix, and in 21:9 there is the Jerusalem Appendix. The women-cities are in striking contrast: a harlot, a pure bride; a ghastly city destroyed, a glorious eternal city; a city fallen, cast down by God, and a city on a mountain, elevated by God; a city from which all keep

their distance, a city to which all desire entry; a city of darkness, a city of light; and so on. By this deliberate comparison, John wishes to move his audience to intentionally choose to live in such a way as to enter the heavenly Jerusalem and enjoy the Lamb's feast. The Christian's real home is in the perfect heavenly city, not in putrid Babylon-Rome.

70. In 21:24 the "nations and the kings of the earth" bring their glory into the heavenly Jerusalem, and in 21:26 the treasures and wealth of the nations are brought there too. In the Old Testament (e.g., Isa 60:3), the consummation of the messianic reign was considered to be the occasion for the conversion of the gentiles (i.e., the nations). At long last, Israel as a light to the nations would be brought into the messianic kingdom, and the nations would convert and enter too. The nations would bring their treasures and gifts in homage to the living God, and Israel would be glorified and vindicated in their eyes. John's point in presenting this parade into the heavenly Jerusalem is to suggest that some of the peoples prophesied and witnessed to by the Church (Rev 10—11) will be converted. God's call for their repentance will be answered. God will be glorified by a universal reign, by a kingdom that includes membership from all peoples, brought into union as his own one flock, a true multicultural diversity in unity. Thus does Revelation express the hope that all persons will be saved.

71. In 22:1–5 the symbolism alludes heavily to the description of earthly paradise in Genesis 2 and 3, and also to the great river in the prophetic vision of the new Jerusalem in Ezekiel 47 to 48. The symbolism is not meant to be taken literally, but to convey the meaning that the heavenly Jerusalem is filled with abundant life, the life of God. In the kingdom of God there is not want, only lavish abundance, that is, it is paradise. Water is a symbol of life, and every city must have water. The water of the heavenly Jerusalem flows from God's throne, the source of life.

Eternal life is the thrust of the scene here; the tree of life in Genesis 2 and 3 is a symbol of immortality.

There is also fullness of life in the heavenly Jerusalem, symbolized in the healing fruit trees. No earthly tree produces fruit perpetually (twelve months a year). Once again the nations are mentioned (22:2), in specific reference to the medicinal use of the trees' leaves. This is not to suggest there is sickness in the heavenly kingdom of God, but rather that God heals and makes whole: there is only fullness of life, whole and abundant in heaven.

The symbolism of paradise, of course, conveys that the heavenly Jerusalem is heaven, where all are blessed and joyful, and in blissful union with God for all eternity. The end of all things is like their beginning, and the similarity between them reflects the divine intent and providence that makes it so.

Revelation 22:6–21

72. Revelation 22:10 recalls 1:3 and 10:4–7. The point here is to emphasize that there is no more delay to the fulfillment of God's salvific plan, announced by his prophets from of old and told in the Gospel. It is also an allusion to Daniel 12:4, where the prophet is told to seal up his book and keep it secret until the end. This allusion serves to underscore that the end has finally arrived. Remember that John has an "already but not yet eschatology," so that the Church since the apostolic era has always lived in the end-times. The nearness of the end must not be thought of as calculable or even necessarily in the current era of human history. Yet the urgency for preparedness for the end is emphasized by not sealing up the book: the end is so imminent that there is hardly time for changing one's ways (22:11). Unlike the scroll given to the Lamb in chapter 5, the book itself is unsealed, although for most people it seems like a completely sealed book.

73. Revelation 22:6 harks back to the book's opening verses (1:1–3), where John says he received the revelation of Jesus Christ to "show his servants what must soon take place." The prophetic Spirit given by God has inspired John to receive and write this work. In the next verse (22:7), there is, as in 1:1–3, a beatitude pronounced over the one who hears John's prophetic message. Clearly John wishes to present his work as prophecy. Those who accept a true prophet's words, since they are God's words, are indeed blessed.

    In 22:10 the words are also described as prophecy. In 22:17 there is an exhortation to hear, which is typical of biblical prophecy ("let everyone who hears..."). We saw a similar prophetic exhortation in the seven letters. Lastly, John himself, the prophet-seer, utters a solemn prophetic warning (22:18) to all who hear the words of his prophecy contained in the book. No one may add to or subtract from his prophecy because it comes from God. Those who do will be punished by the plagues described in the book or lose their share in eternal life. In Deuteronomy 4:2, Moses makes a similar command of his audience. Moses, of course, was also a great servant of God and prophet.

    Given this emphasis by John on this work as prophecy, we can conclude that John sees himself in the line of biblical prophets, moved by the Spirit of God to speak his word to his people, faithfully and clearly. He sees the Book of Revelation as a prophetic apocalypse in the tradition of the Old Testament and early Christian prophets. He wants his work accorded the same status.

74. This list of those excluded from the kingdom is typical of Revelation, but this time contains "dogs." Dog was a derogatory term used by the Israelites of the gentiles (e.g., Mark 7:27–28), since the Jews considered dogs, like the gentiles, to be dirty and contemptible. Evildoers were sometimes punished by having dogs eat them (e.g., Jezebel in 1 Kgs). Here it is adapted to mean those evildoers who are not of the new Israel (and are therefore as unwelcome as the gentiles would

be to the Jews in the biblical world). The other outsiders in this list are those particularly guilty of promoting worship of the Beast and persecuting the Church. Those who "love and practice falsehood" are outside, whereas those who "love and practice truth" are inside.

This is typical of how John has portrayed the two sides of the cosmic struggle: those who worship the Beast are lovers of falsehood (and deceived by Satan); those who worship the Lord are lovers of truth and bear witness to it. Recall that John sees faithful Christians as the "authentic" Jews, and so the ethnic Jews who do not accept Jesus are now logically like "gentile dogs." John often lists outsiders, those who do not get into the kingdom of God, to emphasize that one must live, worship, and love in Christ's truth in order to enter his kingdom. The Christians of the seven letters who were told to repent and did not would be among those who "love and practice falsehood." Once again we see that for John the Church on earth is not synonymous with the heavenly Jerusalem.

75. After promising to come and reward the faithful (22:12–14), Jesus assures the reader that John's prophecy is true, and that it is directed to the churches, not to the inhabitants of the earth or any enemies of God. Revelation is directed to the Church to call it to fidelity. Jesus emphasizes that he himself gave the testimony (witness), and that he himself is *the* Testimony-Witness (the Greek here is *ho martyria*, literally *the* witness, since he is reliable and true). He then assures the reader of his imminent coming, which is also trustworthy. The major point of these final words of Jesus is that they underscore the nature of John's prophecy as the word of Jesus, the Faithful Witness. Jesus is the Witness to divine truth, and anyone wishing to be his disciple must likewise bear this same witness. Faithfully bearing the witness of Jesus is one of Revelation's major overarching themes, and the very reason John is on Patmos (1:1–9). John is a model disciple.

76. At the end of Paul's first letter to the church at Corinth (1 Cor 16:22), the apostle writes "Our Lord, Come," which is very similar to the way Revelation's epistolary epilogue concludes: "Come, Lord Jesus!" This appears to be a liturgical refrain commonly used in the early Church. It is a prayer for the hastening of Christ's coming again in glory. John ends his work in a fashion similar to that of other early Christian apostolic authors. It is fitting that Revelation ends with a series of liturgical outbursts and a final blessing, since it is written from John to the Church in the context of the Lord's day (1:10). It is also appropriate because the deepest longing of every Christian, for which the Christian prays daily, is that "Thy kingdom come."

77. The Book of Revelation is a fitting conclusion to the New Testament, and in fact to the entire Bible, for many reasons. Perhaps one obvious reason is that it forms a theological set of bookends with the first book of the Bible. Genesis considers the beginnings of things and Revelation their end. Genesis introduces salvation history; Revelation concludes it. Revelation is the perfect consummation to the Bible, because it not only is the climax of prophecy but also tells of the fulfillment of all things in Christ. Two major ideas throughout the Bible are covenant and kingdom, which are also intentionally the two major ideas in Revelation. Revelation readdresses these themes in light of Christian life in this world and in the next.

    Another reason has to be that Revelation is so christocentric. Since its overarching theme is the kingdom of God fully consummated in Christ, it is the perfect conclusion to the scriptures. The rest of the New Testament tells of the earthly ministry of Christ, his passion, death, resurrection, and the establishment of his Church. The Old Testament prepares for Christ's first advent (see *Dei Verbum* IV). Revelation completes the narrative by revealing the risen and exalted Christ's place in the cosmos and the meaning of his victory, especially in relation to the Church he established, but also to those outside it as well.

Finally, the theme of God's everlasting covenant with his people as expressed in spousal imagery, a theme that predominates the entire Bible, is brought to fruition here. The old Mosaic covenant is presented this way, and so is the new covenant made in the blood of the Lamb. Revelation gradually builds up to the nuptial feast between the Lamb and his spouse, presenting it as just beginning (19:1–8). The Bride is presented as prepared and ready, awaiting the arrival of her Groom. In fact, she is depicted as crying out in deep longing for the Groom to hasten his advent (22:17–21).

The intimate nuptial union of God and humanity in an everlasting covenant—which is a fundamental and essential concept of both the Old and New Testaments, especially in Revelation—is the Bible's final image. Blessed indeed are those called to the wedding feast of the Lamb (19:9). Even more blessed are those who patiently endure in fidelity to bearing the witness of Jesus so as to be properly attired for the Feast (Matt 22:11–14; Rev 3:4–5; 7:9; 19:8).

Selected Bibliography

Bauckham, R. *The Theology of the Book of Revelation*. Cambridge: Cambridge University Press, 1993.

——— . *The Climax of Prophecy: Studies on the Book of Revelation*. Edinburgh: T & T Clark, 1993.

Caird, G. B. *The Revelation of St. John the Divine*. San Francisco: Harper & Row, 1966.

Catechism of the Catholic Church. 2nd edition. Vatican City: Liberia Editrice Vaticana, 1997.

Charles, R. H. *The Revelation of St. John*. 2 vols. International Critical Commentary. Edinburgh: T & T Clark, 1920.

Collins, A. Y. *Crisis and Catharsis: The Power of the Apocalypse*. Philadelphia: Westminster, 1984.

——— . *The Apocalypse*. New Testament Message 22. Wilmington, DE: Michael Glazier, 1979.

——— . "The Apocalypse (Revelation)." In *The New Jerome Biblical Commentary*, 996–1016. Englewood Cliffs, NJ: Prentice Hall, 1990.

Corsini, E. *The Apocalypse: The Perennial Revelation of Jesus Christ*. Good News Studies 5. Translated by Francis J. Maloney, SDB. Wilmington, DE: Michael Glazier, 1983.

Court, J. M. *Myth and History in the Book of Revelation*. Atlanta: John Knox, 1979.

D'Aragon, J. "The Apocalypse." In *The Jerome Biblical Commentary*, 467–93. Englewood Cliffs, NJ: Prentice Hall, 1968.

Dei Verbum. The Documents of Vatican II, 111–28. Edited by Walter M. Abbot. New York: Guild Press, 1966.

Feuillet, A. *The Apocalypse*. Translated by Thomas Crane. Staten Island, NY: Alba House, 1964.

Harrington, W. *Understanding the Book of Revelation*. Washington, DC: Corpus, 1969.

Irenaeus. *Against Heresies. The Apostolic Fathers with Justin Martyr and Irenaeus.* Ante-Nicene Fathers 1. Edited by A. Roberts and J. Donaldson. Grand Rapids, MI: Eerdmans, 1977.

Jerome. *Hezechielem I.* Corpus Christianorum: Latina LXXV. Edited by F. Glorie. Turnhout, Belgium: Brepols, 1964.

———. *Letter LIII to Paulinus. St. Jerome: Letters and Select Works.* Nicene and Post-Nicene Fathers 6, second series. Edited by P. Schaff and H. Wace. Grand Rapids, MI: Eerdmans, 1954.

Lumen Gentium. The Documents of Vatican II, 14–96. Edited by Walter M. Abbot. New York: Guild Press, 1966.

Koester, Craig R. *Revelation and the End of All Things.* Grand Rapids, MI: Eerdmans, 2001.

Martin, Ralph. *Is Jesus Coming Soon? A Catholic Perspective on the Second Coming.* San Francisco: Ignatius, 1983.

Mathews, S. "The Power to Endure and Be Transformed: Sun and Moon Imagery in Joel and Revelation." In *Imagery and Imagination in Biblical Literature: Essays in Honor of Aloysius Fitzgerald, FSC,* 35–49. Edited by L. Boadt and M. Smith., CBQMS 32. Catholic Biblical Association, Washington, DC: 2001.

———. "Salvific Suffering in John's Apocalypse: The Church as Sacrament of Salvation." In *The Bible on Suffering: Social and Political Implications,* 188–210. Edited by A. Tambasco. New York/Mahwah, NJ: Paulist Press, 2001.

———. "On Patient Endurance: The Suffering of the Faithful in the Book of Revelation." *The Bible Today* 31 (1993): 305–12.

McBride, Alfred. *The Second Coming of Jesus: Meditation and Commentary on the Book of Revelation.* Huntington, IN: Our Sunday Visitor Press, 1993.

Minear, P. *I Saw a New Earth.* Washington, DC: Corpus, 1968.

Olson, Carl E. *Will Catholics Be "Left Behind"? A Catholic Critique of the Rapture and Today's Prophecy Preachers.* San Francisco: Ignatius, 2003.

Schüssler Fiorenza, E. *The Book of Revelation: Justice and Judgment.* Philadelphia: Fortress, 1985.

Skeehan, Patrick W. "King of Kings, Lord of Lords (Apoc 19:16)." *Catholic Biblical Quarterly* 10 (1948): 398.

Sweet, John. *Revelation*. London: SCM, 1979.

Swete, H. B. *The Apocalypse of St. John*. London: Macmillan, 1906.

Thompson, L. L. *The Book of Revelation: Apocalypse and Empire*. Oxford: Oxford University Press, 1990.

Wainwright, Arthur W. *Mysterious Apocalypse: Interpreting the Book of Revelation*. Nashville: Abingdon, 1993.

Witherington, B., III. *Revelation*. NCBC. Cambridge: Cambridge University Press, 2003.